THREE NORTHUMBRIAN POEMS

Cædmon's Hymn, Bede's Death Song
and The Leiden Riddle

EDITED BY

A. H. SMITH, Ph.D.

METHUEN & CO. LTD.

11 NEW FETTER LANE, LONDON EC4

First published in 1933
This edition, with corrections,
first published in 1968

Printed in Great Britain by
Butler & Tanner Ltd, Frome and London

SBN 423 79240 7

2.1

GENERAL EDITORS' PREFACE

IT has often been the complaint of teachers of Old English that the literary materials of the earlier period of literature have been either unavailable in a form suitable for undergraduate use, or incomplete, or inadequately treated. Texts until recently were not always reliable and sometimes represented long traditions of editorial error. The advantages of such a set of texts as this Old English Library will be self-evident to teachers of Old English : the scheme will eventually allow wider scope in the formulation of courses of study, and the separate treatment of each text, however short, is already revealing many new facts both in the establishment of the text and in its interpretation. Besides this, much that has been written on the subject is still widely scattered in the journals, and it is an important part of our work to bring these materials together, often for the first time. These things sometimes tend to swell the apparatus, but readers will readily understand that elaboration of some themes is inevitable.

Apart from the inevitable difference in treatment involved in different texts, we have formulated a general scheme of editing so as to secure a fair agreement in the make-up and apparatus of each volume. Thus, it is a general rule to justify where possible the MS reading and to admit emendations and restorations with hesitation. Textual notes include only variant readings from the MSS and actual deviations in the printed text from the MS. Notes are, for convenience of reference, placed below the text after the textual notes ; glossaries are intended to be complete and we have introduced in them the system of full reference to the grammatical category of each word.

In the texts, there are two points which call for special comment. In the first place, we have disregarded the usage of earlier editors in marking the length of vowels (except where it is so marked in the MS) and of sprinkling the text with brackets and other ingenious devices. The former practice may be useful for scansion, but it is definitely misleading for linguistic purposes ; the abandonment of the latter practice will involve no confusion, for interested readers will find the information they require in the notes below the texts. In the second place, we have gone a step nearer a special Old English fount by the introduction of p ; this is no place to discuss the problem of special founts for older languages, but we hesitated long over our decision. Many inquiries amongst our editors and other scholars revealed a bias in favour of p, and whilst this influenced our decision the responsibility for the adoption of p is ours. The sign ʒ is already widely accepted. In these matters our whole object is to offer intelligible texts as close as possible to the MSS from which they are derived.

In conclusion we would record our thanks to the publishers for their enterprise and practical help, to the printers for the provision of many special characters and for the immeasurable care of their compositors and reader, and to our editors for their willing co-operation and solution of many difficult editorial problems. With the latter we should also couple Professor R. W. Chambers, who with patient forbearance has often submitted himself to our importunate questioning on the duties of editors, and we cannot pass over this chance of expressing our appreciation of all that he has done in the field which we now enter.

A. H. SMITH
F. NORMAN

University College, London
April 1933

PREFACE

THE grouping of these three short poems in one volume is made possible by the nature of the problems involved in their study. These problems have been elaborately treated, but the texts have never before received in a single study that estimate of their literary and historical value which their early date warrants. At the same time an attempt is made to reassess systematically their relative merits as linguistic sources.

The texts are derived either from the manuscripts or from photographs, except that in one or two of the later versions of Cædmon's Hymn and Bede's Death Song, I have relied upon transcripts provided for me by Mr. B. Colgrave and Mr. E. V. Stocks of Durham, my colleague Mrs E. Blackman, and Mr. Alan S. C. Ross of Leeds (who also read through part of my manuscript). A Hereford MS of the Hymn, discovered by Mr. C. B. Judge and pointed out to me by Mr. Ross, I have not dealt with, but it is in the same category as Laud 243 (see p. 3). In the case of the Voss MS, I am greatly indebted to the Leiden University Librarian, who not only allowed me to have the MS at University College, London, for nearly a year, but gave permission for it to be examined under ultra-violet light. The new readings and the confirmation of older readings secured by this means were made possible by Professor E. N. da C. Andrade, who with his assistant freely gave his time to these ends and generously allowed me the use of his apparatus. I would also express my gratitude to Mr. John Wilks, University College Librarian, and Miss N. Beale, who arranged the loan of the MS.

I must also thank my friend, Mr. F. Norman, who read my manuscript and proofs with twofold care in his capacity as general editor. This volume, like the series in general, owes much to his wide knowledge of early Germanic materials and to his stimulating criticism.

A. H. SMITH

CONTENTS

LIST OF ABBREVIATIONS

Archiv .	.	(*Herrigs*) *Archiv für das Studium der neueren Sprachen und Litteraturen*
BDS* .	.	Bede's Death Song
Bülbring	.	K. D. Bülbring, *Altenglisches Elementarbuch*, 1902
Carpenter	.	H. C. A. Carpenter, *Die Deklination in der nordh. Evangelienübersetzung der Lindisfarner Hs*, Bonn 1910
CH* .	.	Cædmon's Hymn
Corpus .	.	The Corpus Glossary (OET 35 ff)
DNB .	.	*The Dictionary of National Biography*
Epinal .	.	The Epinal Glossary (OET 36 ff)
Erfurt .	.	The Erfurt Glossary (OET 36 ff)
ESt .	.	*Englische Studien*
Girvan .	.	R. Girvan, *Angelsaksisch Handboek*, Haarlem 1931
IF .	.	*Indo-Germanische Forschungen*
HE* .	.	Bede's *Historia Ecclesiastica*
Kolbe .	.	T. Kolbe, *Die Konjugation der Lindisfarner Evangelien*, Bonn 1912
Lindelöf	.	U. Lindelöf, *Die südnordhumbrische Mundart*, Bonn 1901
Lindisf .	.	The Lindisfarne Gospels
LR .	.	The Leiden Riddle
Luick .	.	K. Luick, *Historische Grammatik der englischen Sprache*, Leipzig 1921
LVD .	.	Liber Vitae Dunelmensis (Facsimile, Surtees Society ; OET)
MGH .	.	*Monumenta Germaniae Historica*

* Additional letters added to these abbreviations refer to the manuscript variations of the particular text according to the lists on pp. 1–2, 4–5 *infra*.

THREE NORTHUMBRIAN POEMS

THREE NORTHUMBRIAN POEMS

INTRODUCTION

I. Manuscripts

CÆDMON'S HYMN : In the Latin versions of the *Historia Ecclesiastica* (designated HE), Bede, after describing Cædmon's inspiration and the circumstances of the composition of the Hymn (*infra* p. 10) gives a Latin paraphrase of it as :

Nunc laudare debemus auctorem regni caelestis, potentiam Creatoris et consilium illius, facta Patris gloriae. Quomodo ille, cum sit aeternus Deus, omnium miraculorum auctor extitit, qui primo filiis hominum caelum pro culmine tecti, dehinc terram custos humani generis omnipotens creauit. (HE I. xxiv, Plummer i. 259–60)

He then adds a note on translation :

Hic est sensus, non autem ordo ipse uerborum, quae dormiens ille [Caedmon] canebat ; neque enim possunt carmina, quamuis optime conposita, ex alia in aliam linguam ad uerbum sine detrimento sui decoris ac dignitatis transferri.

In its Old English form, therefore, the Hymn is not an integral part of Bede's *Historia* ; in such manuscripts as contain it, it is usually added in the margin or at the foot of the appropriate page, or, as in the Moore manuscript, on some other page.

In the manuscripts of the Old English version of Bede's HE (designated OEBede) the Hymn itself replaces the paraphrase and Bede's note on his translation, no longer appropriate, is omitted.

There are four manuscripts of HE which contain the Hymn in a Northumbrian form. These are :

M : Cambridge University Library, Kk 5, 16 (the Moore MS) at the top of the last page (fol. 128b) ; for date cf *infra* p. 20 ; for facsimile and editions *v*. Bibliography.

L: Leningrad Public Library, Q.v.I. 18, fol. 107b; for date cf *infra* p. 19, and for references to this important MS cf Bibliography.

D: Dijon Public Library 547 (334), fol. 59b, twelfth century.

P: Paris, Cod. Lat. 5237, fol. 72, early fifteenth century ; these two MSS were discovered by P. Wuest and edited and described by him in ZfdA xlviii. 205 ff.

Besides these, there are seven manuscripts of HE (one now lost) which contain the Hymn in a later form, as well as five of the OEBede (one seriously damaged by fire).[1] A detailed study of nine of the manuscripts was made by Wuest (*op. cit.*), whose discovery of D and P confirmed the view held by Zupitza (ZfdA xxii. 222) that the forms of the Hymn found in the OEBede were derived from a current copy that differed in important particulars from the only Northumbrian version known at that time (M), but Wuest's suggestion that *Y (his reconstructed prototype of D and P) is as old as M, possibly more authentic,[2] and that *Y is the source of the OEBede versions is improbable, as Frampton shows. The latter's conclusion that M is superior in age and authenticity is strongly corroborated by the more recent discovery of L, which is almost as archaic as M (cf *infra* p. 20).

From the list of variants (*infra* p. 38) it will be seen that D and P agree very closely and are derived from a common prototype (*Y) distinct from M and L, and that the most significant textual variant is *eordu* (line 5) in DP for

[1] The late version printed below is from Hatton 43 (Bodleian Library), fol. 129a bottom margin, tenth century, printed by A. S. Napier in MLN iv. 275–6 ; Winchester Cathedral 3 (printed by Plummer ii. 252 and M. G. Frampton in MPh xxii. opp. p. 3) is slightly older but somewhat defective. An HE version is chosen for the purposes of linguistic comparison. Other versions printed in full are Bodleian Library 163 (eleventh century) by M. G. Frampton 5 note, Laud 243 (twelfth century) by J. Stevenson in *The Church Historians of England* (London 1853) ; the OEBede MS Tanner 10 (Bodleian Library) by T. Miller ii. 344. Frampton also gives the significant variants of all MSS except L in his detailed account of the relationships (*op. cit.*).

[2] For Wuest's reconstruction of *Y cf ZfdA xlviii. 219, and on its date (Wuest suggests c. 750) and dialect cf *infra* p. 36, §§ 19, 20.

aelda in ML. With the exception of one manuscript (Laud 243) [1] all later versions of the Hymn in HE manuscripts follow ML in reading *ylda*, whilst the OEBede manuscripts follow DP in reading *eorþan*. Two other differences, however, do not appear to support this division. ML line 9 have *firum foldu* and the OEBede has the normal *firum foldan* for this ; DP have *firum on/ol foldu* and the HE versions have *firum on foldum*. But in *firum on foldum* we have an unparalleled use of *folde* in the plural [2] and it may well be that the scribe of the prototype of this group read *foldu* (on which both ML and DP agree) as *foldũ* or as an error for the dat. pl. and he himself then independently added the preposition to govern his new dative *foldum*. This in effect would mean that the prototype of the OEBede group was not *Y itself but a predecessor of *Y which still lacked *on* and read *firum foldu*, and that *Y independently added *on* and gave rise to no other versions but D and P. [3]

The other important difference is that DP have *we* (line 1), but ML omit it. The later versions give no indication of the original reading, for two manuscripts of the OEBede (which in respect of reading *eorþan* follow DP) omit *we*, whilst the remaining manuscripts, both HE and OEBede, insert it. It is probable that *we* was added independently (like *on*) in the prototype of the later HE

[1] This version differs from other later HE versions in reading *eorðe* for *ylda*, *gehwæs* for *gehwylc* and *teode* for *tida*, and so agrees with the OEBede versions, but the omission of *ord onstealde*, the reading *on folden* for *on foldum* and the transference of *halig scyppend* to the end support Frampton's view that the scribe wrote it from memory and had in mind a form akin to that in the OEBede. It is therefore excluded from the HE MSS in the discussion.

[2] OE *folde* is found in the plur. (e.g. Ps. 64/6), but only in the sense ' territorial division, country ', a meaning not warranted in this context.

[3] In any case *firum on foldu* is a possible reading if we take *on foldu* as qualifying *firum* with *foldu* as dat. sg., but in early Nb there are no instances of a dat. sg. in -*u* (in *n*-stems), yet that may be due to the poverty of early Nb texts. In later Nb such forms are occasionally found.

group (for they also agree in reading *gehwilc* for *gehwæs* and *tida* for *teode*), but otherwise we must suppose that addition or omission of *we* depended largely upon individual scribes. In early Northumbrian such pronouns were sometimes omitted,[1] as in ML, and the fact that DP have *we* but that two of the related OEBede versions omit it rather indicates that *we* was in *Y but not in *Y's prototype from which the OEBede versions are ultimately derived.

The ultimate prototype of *Y (= DP) and of the OEBede versions, therefore, appears to have differed from ML only in the reading *eorðu* for *aelda*. That ML represent most closely the version known to Bede is proved by his paraphrase (*filiis hominum*), but the ultimate relationship of the earliest prototype of *Y and the OEBede version with ML cannot be determined; each has equal claims to represent Cædmon's actual composition.

BEDE'S DEATH SONG: Bede's Death Song is found only in manuscripts of Cuthbert's letter to Cuthwin, describing Bede's last days and death. This letter is usually found as an addition to Bede's HE, but it is also found as Book I, chapter xv, of Symeon of Durham's *Historia Dunelmensis Ecclesiæ*, written between 1104 and 1109.[2] Some manuscripts of the letter as found in HE omit the whole passage relating to the Death Song, others omit the Song only. The oldest manuscript is St Gall Codex 254, p. 253, written in ninth-century Carolingian minuscules (cf *infra* p. 23). Closely related to this version (A), there are four other continental manuscripts, which have been examined and printed by Professor R. Brotanek (*Texte und Untersuchungen* 151 ff):

[1] Cf G. Sarrazin, ESt xxxviii. 183 ff. The addition of *we* is more likely than its omission in later recensions and there was, as Frampton, *op. cit.* 9, shows, a strong tendency to begin OE poetry with a pronoun (e.g. *Beowulf, Exodus, Daniel*, &c.). The ' modernizing ' tendency is noticed also in later versions in the substitution of *ord* for the earlier *or* (MLDP) (cf Frampton 6).

[2] *Symeonis monachi opera omnia*, ed. T. Arnold (Rolls Series) I. xix.

B: Bamberg (Königl. Bibliothek) A. i. 47, fol. 21a, 11th century (Brotanek 152, 171);

E: Stift Heiligenkreuz, Codex 12, fol. 170b, 12th century (*op. cit.* 153, 173);

I: Chorherrenstift Klosterneuburg, 787, fol. 185a, 13th century (*op. cit.* 154, 173);

L: München, Codex 14603, fol. 138, 16th century, (*op. cit.* 155, 174).

These continental versions agree very closely with A (St Gall), and spellings like *neid-, uuiurthit, hiniongae, deothdaege,* indicate that all are derived from a common prototype. Professor Brotanek (*op. cit.* 175) supposes (1) that there was a single continental prototype with *uuiurthit* due to Old High German influence, and (2) that there were two branches of this, one reading *thaere* or *thare,* which survived in B as *thae,* and the other reading *there,* which survives in A as *the'* and from A we have copies E I L reading *the* (omitting the abbreviation mark). But *uuiurthit* is capable of another interpretation (*infra* p. 27, § 2) and there is some doubt whether A *the'* should be interpreted *there* or *them.* Professor Brotanek's determination of the relationship depends on the assumption that older *ae* was later written *e*—a usual change in Latin orthography—and there is other evidence in support of it in forms like EIL *gaste* for AB *gastae, aeththa* for OE *eððe,* &c. But there is one case, where a supposed derivative of A, namely E, has *się* against *sie* in A B I L. This reduces the value of *the'*—*thae* as a critical variant, and it is possible that B's *thae* (for *thae' = thaem*) is a scribal variant of *the* (for *the' = them*). At the same time, this does not alter the fact that in these versions we have a very closely related family.

The remaining manuscripts, all English, are twelfth-century or later, and the only important variant, *heonen* for *daege* in the last line, shows that the versions found in HE manuscripts (Stowe 114, fol. 112b, Digby 211, fol. 108a, &c.) and those found in Symeon of Durham (Durham, Bishop Cosin's Library, p. 56, Cotton, Faustina A V, fol. 42a, &c.) are more closely related to each other than to the St Gall group.[1] Other differences, such as the substitution of gen. sg. *ðances* for *thonc-* and of *ge-* for *ymb-*, point to the same thing. With one exception the Symeon of Durham versions agree almost letter for letter, and it is reasonable to suppose that Symeon of Durham derived his version from some manuscript of the letter akin to that found in the HE manuscripts. The existence of three different recensions of the Song is also suggested by the textual variations in the letter itself. St Gall, for instance, differs from the rest in reading *dicens . . . corpore* (cf *infra* p. 42) ; the Symeon of Durham version differs from the rest in adding *hoc est Anglica* as well as in the addition of a Latin translation of the Song, to mention but a few points. One exception to this agreement between the Latin texts and the English texts is the Symeon of Durham manuscript B.M. Titus A II ; so far as the Latin goes this follows closely the Symeon version, but in its orthography the Song agrees more closely with the later HE group, though in some respects it may represent a slightly older tradition as in *weorðeð* (unmutated) for *wyrþeð* in other manuscripts, *-hycgenne* for *hicgen(n)e*, *weorðe* for *wurðe*. Except for the first two letters *Fo* the Song was here added by a second scribe.

The material is not sufficient to enable us to say with any certainty whether these late versions are of Northern origin or not. In the version printed *infra* p. 43 *weorðeð* is non-West Saxon ; it may be an adaptation of *uuiurthit* ; on the other hand, in all the rest *wyrþeð* certainly is West Saxon (except for *-eð*), as is *wurðe*. But in such cases it is not necessary to assume an earlier West Saxon prototype, as these may simply be orthographic forms of ' standard ' Old English, possibly due in part to Symeon of Durham himself, who was probably of Southern origin. They can hardly represent the dialect of Durham in the twelfth century, for there we should rather expect the forms

[1] For a complete list of MSS and textual variants, *v.* R. Brotanek, *op. cit.* 151 *et passim*). T. Arnold in his edition of Symeon's works prints a version from B.M. Faustina A V.

worðeð and *worðe*.[1] There is nothing, therefore, to show in what way precisely these later versions of the Song are related to the St Gall version. The letter, however, was known on the continent two or more centuries before it was current in England, and it is not unlikely that the English versions of the Song are derived from some continental manuscript closely related to St Gall and introduced into England,[2] for the presence or absence of Cuthbert's letter in English manuscripts of Bede has no connexion with the textual history of the HE, and its inclusion must have been by contamination.

LEIDEN RIDDLE: The Leiden Riddle is preserved in the Leiden University Manuscript, Cod. Voss 106, on the lower half of the last page, fol. 25b. The manuscript includes a single leaf (fol. 1), probably inserted in recent times, giving the names of the popes from Lucius to Simmachus with details of the ordinations they performed. The rest of the manuscript is in one hand (Carolingian minuscules of the ninth century, cf *infra* p. 23, with slight traces of English influence in the dotted surrounds of some of the capitals). On fol. 2a is part of a Greek litany, on fols. 2b to 8b the Latin Riddles of Symphosius; on fols. 9a to 10a a list of Aldhelm's Riddles,[3] which follow on fol. 10b.[4] The last of Aldhelm's Riddles (*De Creatura*) ends

---

[1] A discussion of the language of these later versions of the Death Song will be published elsewhere.

[2] If this were not so, we should expect to find the letter in one or another of the various earlier English MSS of the HE. We might have had confirmation of it if the identity of Cuthwin, the recipient of the letter, were known.

[3] The riddles of Symphosius are printed in Migne's *Patrologia Latina* vii. 285 (there ascribed to Lactantius) and those of Aldhelm in Giles, *Aldhelmi Opera* (Oxford 1844); the best critical edition is Ehwald, *Aldhelmi Opera* (MGH, Auct. Ant. xv.).

[4] On fol. 10a after the list of Aldhelm's riddles are some glosses *Nimphae aelfinni eadem et muse : oreades duun-aelfinni, driades uudu-aelfinne, amadriades uaeter-* (MS *uaꝺer-*) *aelfinn', maides feld-aelfinne, naides sae-aelfinne.* Printed by Bethman in ZfdA v. 199. They are extant in a later form in a larger glossary (Wright-Wülcker, *Vocabularies* i. 189). The words are not recorded in Bosworth-Toller from this Leiden source.

on fol. 25b followed by a brief epilogue (*Expliciunt enigmata* &c.)[1] and in the remaining space the scribe has added the Old English riddle, *Mec se ueta uonʒ*.[2] This Old English is in a poor condition, due partly to stains, partly to chafing, and to some extent through the use of a stylus to mark the guide lines which, through roughening of the parchment, prevented the pen making firm clear lines—the Old English being rather smaller than the preceding Latin. O. Schlutter (Anglia xxxii. 384) is of the opinion that other writing on the parchment was erased before the Old English was added. But whatever the cause, the parts most affected are the right-hand side and the last two lines, and it is chiefly in these places where difficulty has always been experienced in reading the manuscript. This has to a small extent been aggravated by the use of a reagent in 1864 (cf *infra* p. 9) ; it is now extremely doubtful whether further research on the manuscript will produce a more reliable text than Sweet's or Kern's, but by ultra-violet light it has been possible to confirm previous readings and to place beyond doubt other readings which are uncertain without such help. Even so some letters remain illegible. For this reason consideration should be given to F. Dietrich's edition and lithographed facsimile (made in 1859–60) as this was the last transcript made before the application of a reagent.[3] W. G. Pluy-

---

[1] Printed by Ehwald 149 from a Paris Codex ; cf also Dietrich, *Kynewulfi Poetae Aetas* 17.

[2] A point worthy of notice is that the end of a MS line always coincides with the end of a verse-line or half-line, except on line 7 of the MS which ends at *mith*, the remaining words of the verse-line being written on the previous line. But there is room for *heliðum* at any rate after *mith* though that space was left blank. If this arrangement is not mere chance, the best explanation is that the scribe was faithfully copying the line arrangement of his original, where no doubt line 7, probably taking up more room than in the extant MS, left no space for the remaining words of the verse-line. Cf *infra* p. 25n.

[3] An earlier edition than Dietrich's was Bethmann's (ZfdA v. 199), but this is a poor and careless transcript. Dietrich's text was the basis of that in M. Rieger's *Alt- u. angelsächsisches Lesebuch* (Giessen 1861).

gers' transcript made in 1864 with the aid of a reagent is also of value as being a purely objective text. His transcript was inserted at the end of the manuscript with the note *Descripsi in Novembr.* 1864. *Medicinam adhibui: sulphuret. ammonii. W.G.P.* With the assistance of these it is possible to consider the manuscript objectively up to a certain point, and thereafter confirmation may be sought in Aldhelm's Latin riddle *De Lorica* and the Exeter Book riddle no. 35.

Aldhelm's riddle *De Lorica* is the immediate source of the Leiden Riddle, which is a fairly close but not literal translation of it. The text of the Latin riddle from the Leiden manuscript (fol. 14a) is:

> Roscida me genuit gelido de uiscere tellus ;
> Non sum setigero lanarum uellere facta,
> Licia nulla trahunt nec garrula fila resultant
> Nec crocea seres texunt lanugine uermes
> Nec radiis carpor duro nec pectine pulsor ;
> Et tamen en uestis uulgi sermone uocabor;
> Spicula non uereor longis exempta faretris.

The last line provides us with the substance of the last defective line of the Leiden Riddle.

The West Saxon version is found in the Exeter Book fols. 109a–109b, in a form which agrees closely with that of the Leiden manuscript. Apart from grammatical and phonological differences due to age and dialect, the main variations are the change of number in *hrutende, wyrda,* the substitution of *scripeð* sg. for *scelfath* pl., the reversal of *aam sceal* to *sceal amas,* the insertion of *mon,* and the replacement of the last two lines by two others. For the text *v. infra* p. 45.

There have been since Pluygers' time several independent re-examinations of the manuscript, by H. Sweet (OET 150–1), O. Schlutter (Anglia xxxii. 384, xxxiii. 457) and J. H. Kern (Anglia xxxiii. 453, and xxxviii. 261). All differ from each other in a few points but Dr. Schlutter's text, which has been adopted wholly or in part in A. J. Wyatt's *Old English Riddles* 92, Fr. Tupper's *Riddles of the Exeter*

Book and C. T. Onions' edition of Sweet's *Anglo-Saxon Reader*, differs from the rest in other important points (cf *infra* p. 44, notes *passim*). The mere fact that there is disagreement amongst editors proves how inadequate the evidence of the manuscript might be and the fact that Dr. Schlutter's second text varies from his first [1] shows how personal the interpretation can be. The text in this volume has been arrived at under better conditions than were possible for previous editors, and with one or two exceptions it agrees more with Professor Kern's and Sweet's than with Dr. Schlutter's. The readings of these editors are recorded in the notes (*infra* p. 44 ff) but generally without discussion unless the weight of opinion is against the reading adopted.

II. AUTHORSHIP

CÆDMON'S HYMN : The name *Caedmon* is of British origin [2] and this has been taken to imply that Cædmon himself was a Briton or of British extraction. But the survival of such British personal names in Anglian Northumbria was not uncommon [3] and all that they show is that there had once been a fairly close contact between the native Britons and the invading Angles in that district.

The only biographical information we have about Cædmon is recorded in Bede's *Historia Ecclesiastica* (Book IV. cap. xxiv). There we learn that in the monastery of Hild (abbess 657–80) at *Strenæshalc* [4] a certain brother

---

[1] Thus *eorðuong* replaces *erðuong*, *hyʒidohta* replaces *huʒidohta*, *ðreavun-* replaces *ðreaun-*, *cam a* replaces *caam* and *lon(gum)* at the end is omitted.

[2] British *Catumannos*, cf M. Förster, *Keltisches Wortgut* 179 ; A. S. Cook (MLA vi. 9 ff) prefers a Hebrew derivation and thinks the name may have been suggested by Genesis xv. 19.

[3] Cf M. Förster, *op. cit.* 176 ff, and A. H. Smith, *Place-Names of the North Riding* xvi.

[4] *Strenæshalc* has by long tradition been identified with Whitby. The Memorial of The Foundation of Whitby Abbey (Surtees Society, vol. lxix. 1) speaks of the place *qui olim Streoneshalc, deinde Prestebi, nunc vero Witebi vocatur* ; so too Symeon of Durham (Rolls Series) I. 111. In the eleventh century the monastery of

had lived in the secular habit until he was well advanced
in years, never having learned anything of the art of versi-
fying, and, lacking that skill, he usually left those enter-
tainments (at which for the sake of mirth each should sing)
as his turn came round. On one such occasion he went
out to the stable where that night he was in charge of the
horses and at the proper time he went to sleep. "But
someone appeared to him in his sleep and addressing him
by name said, 'Cædmon, sing me something.' But he
replying said, 'I know not how to sing ; that is why I
left the entertainment and came here, for I could not sing.'
He who spoke with him then said, 'Nevertheless, you
shall sing.' He replied, 'What must I sing ? ' And the
other said, 'Sing of the beginnings of created things.'
Thereupon Cædmon began to sing to the praise of God
verses he had never heard." Here Bede gives a paraphrase
of the Hymn (*supra* p. 1) and adds that, on waking, Cædmon
remembered all that he had sung. In the morning he
related this to the steward, and after being taken to the
abbess he was commanded to tell of his dream and to
repeat the verses ; it was concluded that heavenly grace
had been conferred upon him and the abbess instructed
him to enter the monastic life. He was then taught sacred
history and this he converted into the most harmonious
verse. "He sang of the creation of the world and of the
origin of the human race and the whole history of Genesis ;
he sang of the departure of Israel from Egypt and of the
entry into the promised land, and of many other histories
from Holy Scripture—the Incarnation, the Passion, Resur-
rection and Ascension into Heaven, the coming of the Holy
Spirit and the teaching of the Apostles." [1] He was a very

Hild was in ruins, having been destroyed, according to the Memorial
' by the most cruel pirates Ingwar and Ubba ', the Danish leaders.
William of Malmesbury says that he does not describe the abbeys
of the north because the old ones are all in ruins and the new ones
have not yet achieved fame (c. 1125, *Gesta Pontificium* 254).
[1] The problem of Cædmon's authorship of the so-called Cæd-
monian poems (Genesis, &c.) is briefly and carefully summarized
by H. Bradley (DNB s.n. *Cædmon*) and in more recent years, when

religious man, humbly submitting himself to discipline, yet zealous against those who would do otherwise. At length after an illness of fourteen days he died. The date of his death has been variously assigned to 670, 676, and 680, but on this point we have no information at all. All we know is that Cædmon was advanced in years when he entered the monastery and that happened during the abbacy of Hild, between 657 and 680. His body, according to William of Malmesbury, writing about 1125, had then lately been discovered with those of other notable people at Whitby and had been moved to a place of honour.[1]

In view of his accuracy and skill as an historian there can be little doubt that Bede believed the hymn to be Cædmon's; if he followed his usual practice, he had it from some trustworthy source, either an eyewitness or some written description made by such an eyewitness at Whitby. It is not known whether Bede had ever been at *Strenæshalc*, but we know that he visited York in 733 [2] and he may have been in Yorkshire before the *Historia Ecclesiastica* was written. And a connexion with *Strenæshalc* is clearly suggested by Bede's use of a Life of Gregory the Great, without doubt composed by a Whitby monk.[3] But it was formerly held that the hymn as we have it is simply a translation of Bede's paraphrase [4] and so is not Cædmon's own composition, and that the whole story of Cædmon is fictitious.[5] The former of these views was strongly refuted by Zupitza (ZfdA xxii. 217 ff) : not only

the prevailing tendency is to accept the Cædmon authorship, by Sir I. Gollancz, *The Cædmon Manuscript* lx. and G. P. Krapp, *The Junius Manuscript* xxvii.

[1] *Inventaque sunt noviter et in eminentiam elata sanctorum corpora, Trumwini episcopi, Oswii regis, . . . et illius monachi quem divino munere scientiam cantus accepisse Beda refert:* Gesta Pontificium (Rolls Series) 254.

[2] *Epistola ad Ecgbertum* (Plummer's Bede I. 405).

[3] Plummer, *op. cit.* II. 389.

[4] J. J. Conybeare, *Illustrations of Anglo-Saxon Poetry* 6 ff and R. Wülcker, PBB iii. 348 ff.

[5] Sir F. Palgrave in *Archæologia* xxiv. 341.

is the oldest version of the Hymn in the Moore manuscript almost contemporary with Bede, but in style it clearly antedates the Latin version : the equation of *terram* with both *middunʒeard* and *foldu*, of *creauit* with *scop* and *tiadæ*, and *cum sit aeternus deus* with *eci dryctin* shows that it is the Latin and not the Old English which has lost *decor* and *dignitas* (cf *supra* p. 1) in the translation. We cannot therefore doubt that Bede was actually paraphrasing a poem already in existence. The second view that the whole Cædmon story is ' a tale floating on the breath of tradition ' was put forward by Sir F. Palgrave on the ground of a close parallel to the story in two Latin fragments, *Præfatio in librum antiquum lingua Saxonica conscriptum* and *Versus de Poeta*.[1] In the *Præfatio* it is stated that Louis the Pious (emperor 814–40) desired his subjects to be supplied with a version of the Scriptures and so " he instructed a certain Saxon poet of no small renown to render the Old and New Testaments into German ". These imperial commands the poet readily obeyed. The *Præfatio* then adds that this same bard, who had hitherto been ignorant of the poetic art, had been commanded in his sleep to turn the precepts of the sacred law into a song in his own language. In the *Versus de Poeta* the story of the inspiration is told in greater detail. Weary and over-come by sleep after pasturing the cattle, the man gave himself up to rest. Soon a divine voice echoed from heaven, ' O, what dost thou do ? Why dost thou waste the time of song ? Begin to recite the divine laws and translate them into thine own tongue.' And thus the simple peasant became a poet. But neither of these stories, which are usually held to refer to the Old Saxon *Heliand*, is entirely independent of Bede's account of Cædmon ;

---

[1] The extant versions are derived from the *Catalogus testium veritatis* of Flacius Illyricus, printed in 1562 ; their genuineness and antiquity are proved by the occurrence of the word *uittea* (OE *fitt* ' poem ') " which no renaissance scholar could have hit upon ". They are accessible in E. Sievers' *Heliand* 3–6 and Plum-mer's *Bede* II. 255.

the verbal resemblances are at times close,[1] and as they are not independent it cannot be proved that this particular story of poetic inspiration existed in folk-tradition and that Bede's account was adapted from this fictitious source.

The main fact that Cædmon composed the Hymn there is no need to doubt, for in more recent times it has not been uncommon for peasants to compose verse of great merit in their native dialect, but the originality is less in the verse-forms than in subject matter and diction. The supernatural explanation of Cædmon's poetic inspiration was probably suggested by Bede or by Bede's informants or by other stories, to show why an aged farmhand had been endowed with the faculty of composing verse. Yet doubt of a divine inspiration does not imply that neither the poet nor his work was real. Such stories are told of Pindar, Hesiod, Homer and Aeschylus and of the Icelander Hallbjǫrn.[2] Thus, " Aeschylus said that whilst watching grapes as a boy he fell asleep in a field, and Dionysus appeared to him and bade him write tragedy. In the morning, wishing to obey the god, he tried and found that he composed verses with ease."[3] Similarly, Hallbjǫrn, a shepherd, had long wished to sing the praises of the dead poet Þorleif, but he was unable to do so until Þorleif appeared to him one night and unloosed his tongue.[4] The account of Cædmon's inspiration may have followed some such story, but there is no reason why it should not have arisen independently in Northumbria where tales of miracles were no less common than elsewhere.

In its relationship with the rest of Old English poetry Cædmon's Hymn appears to display no great originality,

---

[1] Plummer, *l.c.*, and Sievers xxv ff.

[2] Cf J. Grimm, *Deutsche Mythologie* (1854) 859 and III. 276 (J. S. Stallybrass's translation III. 905–6, IV. 1583), where some of these stories are collected. They have since been noted by Plummer II. 254, F. Klaeber in MLN xlii. 390 and L. Pound in *Studies presented to F. Klaeber* 232.

[3] Pausanias, *Description of Greece* I. xxi, cited by Grimm, *l.c.* and Mrs Aurner in MLN xli. 535.

[4] *Fornmanna Sǫgur* iii. 102 (Grimm, *l.c.*).

for, though it is technically accurate, nine or more of its eighteen half-lines can be paralleled in other poems.[1] But in Cædmon's time when Northumbria had been converted to Christianity for only half a century these phrases belonging to Christian poetry could scarcely have become conventional, as they certainly were in later Old English ; on the contrary, the poem represents the beginnings of such a diction and its freshness and originality must have been felt a generation or more after its composition ; no mere assembling of clichés would have called for inspiration, divine or otherwise.

BEDE'S DEATH SONG : The greater part of the information we have about Bede [2] is found in the notice of himself and his works with which he concludes the *Historia Ecclesiastica*. There he tells us that he was born (about 672) in the territory of the monastery of Wearmouth and Jarrow, in which he spent all but the first seven years of his life. He was, therefore, both by birth and residence a Northumbrian. He became deacon when he was nineteen and was admitted to the priesthood when he was thirty.[3] He never sought preferment, but spent his life in teaching and literary work. Almost the whole of Bede's extant works are in Latin and the greatest of these is his *Historia Ecclesiastica* which he completed in 731, when he was in his fifty-ninth year. But Bede also made contributions of his own to native literature, though with one exception these have not survived. Thus, on account

---

[1] Line 1b in Gen. 1363, &c. ; 2a in Sat. 353 ; 4a and 8a in Beow. 108, *et freq.* ; 4b in Riddle 3 (59), Beow. 2407, &c. ; 5b in Beow. 70, 150, &c. ; 6a cf Phoen. 173 ; 7b in Gen. 2757, &c. ; 9b in Gen. 5, 116, &c., Jud. 301 ; cf Grein, *Sprachschatz der angelsächsischen Dichter* (*passim*, s.vv.).

[2] The personal name in OE is *Baeda* (*Bæda*) or *Beda* (cf M. Redin, *Uncompounded Personal Names in Old English* 60). In Latin contexts it is usually *Beda*, gen. *Bedae* (*Bede*), though occasionally the OE weak gen. *Bedan* is used (*Epist : Karolinum aevum* (MGH) I. 347), and this weak gen. is also Latinized to *Bedani* (*op. cit.*).

[3] For a good account of Bede's Life and works *v.* Plummer I. i *et passim*.

of the frequent ignorance of Latin amongst the monks, he translated the Creed and the Lord's Prayer into English,[1] he was interested enough to describe and praise Cædmon's work (*supra* p. 10), and he himself was, according to Cuthbert, skilled in vernacular poetry.[2] So, too, when overcome by illness before his death in 735 [3] he laboured to complete his translation into English of the Gospel of Saint John and some of the works of Isidore.[4] The only one of his English compositions extant is the song which he composed on his death-bed and which Cuthbert quotes in his letter to Cuthwin giving in great detail a description of Bede's last days. The Death Song is without doubt authentic, for Cuthbert was one of the brethren of the monastery [5] and the letter is clearly the work of such an eyewitness. Cuthbert himself asserts at the end of his letter that "many things might be told and written about him, but my unskilful tongue makes my words brief, but later I intend to write more fully concerning him what I have seen with my eyes and heard with my ears", whilst the plain fact that Bede was in failing health a short while before his death yet able to continue his literary work is vouched for by Bede himself in his letter to Ecgbert, Archbishop of York (Nov. 734), where he states that he is unable to visit Ecgbert *uerum quia hoc ne fieret, superueniens, ut nosti, corporis mei ualitudo prohibuit.*[6] There is less need to question Cuthbert's veracity than there is to doubt the authenticity of Bede's own

---

[1] *Epistola ad Ecgbertum* (Plummer's *Bede* i. 409).

[2] Cuthbert's Letter to Cuthwine (*infra* p. 42).

[3] On the date of Bede's death cf Plummer I. lxxi.

[4] Convenient editions of the whole of Cuthbert's letter will be found in Bede's *Historia Eccles.* ed. Mayor and Lumby 399, Plummer I. clx (and translation ib. lxxii) and Symeon of Durham (Rolls Series) I. 43.

[5] A *Cuthbercht* is mentioned as a priest in *Liber Vitae Dunelm.* as also is *Beda* (Surtees Soc. Facsimile fol. 18b). *Cuthberct* was afterwards Abbot of Wearmouth and Jarrow (ib. 16b) and he is the man who sent Lullus copies of Bede's works (*infra* p. 24).

[6] Plummer I. 405.

narrative of Cædmon. On Cuthbert's testimony the Death Song is Bede's. Its thought is in keeping with the occasion as with his other sayings at that time, and in the simplicity and directness of its language it has the marks of spontaneity. That it has been preserved may be due in the first place to nothing more than the fortunate presence of the writing materials which the boy Wilberct had in the chamber for transcribing Bede's translation of the Gospel of Saint John.

THE LEIDEN RIDDLE: The Leiden Riddle holds a position between Aldhelm's Latin riddle *De Lorica* on the one hand and the Exeter Book version on the other (*supra* p. 9), but it is difficult, if not impossible, to determine exactly how the close dependence of each version upon its predecessor came about. The differences between the two Old English versions (*supra* p. 9) are such as might normally arise through a long oral tradition, and the grammatical error in line 8 of the West Saxon version and the replacement of the last two lines make it certain that this version is a later recension of a form closely akin to the Leiden version. In these respects, as well as in date (*infra* pp. 23, 37), the Leiden Riddle is nearer the Latin original. It is one of the two Old English riddles which are held to be translations of Latin riddles,[1] in both cases Aldhelm's, and its inclusion at the end of a manuscript of the latter much in the same way as glosses were added to fill blank spaces suggests that it was in conception a literary exercise, though a successful one. The identity of the poet-translator is unknown, and though in its extant form the Leiden Riddle is Northumbrian, we do not know that the translator was a Northumbrian. Aldhelm, the author of the Latin original, was a West Saxon,

---

[1] The other is no. 40 in the Exeter Book riddles (the Creation). On the history of the Latin riddles and their relationship to the Old English ones *v.* F. Tupper's *Riddles of the Exeter Book* (Introd. *passim*) and A. J. Wyatt's *Old English Riddles* (Introd.), and on cultural aspects *v.* E. von Erhardt-Siebold, *Die Lateinischen Rätsel der Angelsachsen* (Anglist. Forschungen no. 61).

being a near relative, possibly the son, of Centwine, king of Wessex. He was born about 639 and was educated during the early part of his life at Malmesbury under the Irish scholar Maeldubh, and later at Canterbury under Archbishop Theodore and Abbot Hadrian. In 675 he returned to his native place as its first abbot and from 705 until his death four years later he was first bishop of the new see of Sherborne.[1] Although he had spent his life in the south, his works were known far outside Wessex: Bede was familiar with his great work *De Virginitate* and with his 'notable book against the error of the Britons in not celebrating Easter at the proper time'[2] and says of him that 'he had a clean style and was remarkable for his ecclesiastical and liberal erudition', whilst his *Epistola ad Acircium* (written c. 695),[3] in which the riddles are incorporated, was addressed to Aldfrid, king of Northumbria, himself a great scholar. It is not improbable, therefore, that the translation of the riddle *De Lorica* was first made in Northumbria. At the same time it is not beyond the limits of possibility that Aldhelm himself was the translator, for William of Malmesbury on the authority of the lost *Manualem librum Regis Elfredi* says that Aldhelm did not neglect the songs of his native tongue and that Ælfred the Great, to whom his vernacular songs were known, thought that he was without equal in the composition of English poetry.[4] The translation is the work of such a poet. But if that poet were Aldhelm, or indeed any West Saxon, we should have to assume that his verse

[1] On Aldhelm's life cf the life by Faricius (Migne's *Patrologia Latina* vol. 89, 63 ff) and William of Malmesbury's *Gesta Pontificium* Book V (Rolls Series). Cf also M. Manitius, *Aldhelm u. Baeda* (Vienna 1886), DNB s.n. and M. R. James, *Two Ancient English Scholars* (David Murray Foundation Lecture), Glasgow 1931.

[2] Bede, HE Book V, cap. xviii. The second work referred to is Aldhelm's letter to Gerontius ; both works are included in Ehwald's edition.

[3] M. Manitius, *Lateinische Literatur des Mittelalters* I. 136 (with references).

[4] *Gesta Pontificium* (Rolls) 336.

was quickly turned into Northumbrian so carefully that no trace of the supposed original dialect remains. That in itself is not a serious objection, for in other short poems like Cædmon's Hymn or Bede's Death Song where the original dialect was Northumbrian, the later West Saxon versions do not betray it.

III.   DATE AND LOCALIZATION OF THE EXTANT TEXTS

Of the extant versions of the three poems only the two older ones of Cædmon's Hymn can be dated on other than linguistic grounds ; of none of them have we any exact and independent knowledge of the place and circumstances of their origin. But in each case we have a *terminus a quo* in the date of composition : Cædmon's Hymn was probably composed about 660–80, and Bede's Death Song in 735, whilst the Leiden Riddle cannot antedate the composition of the *Epistola ad Acircium* about 695. The other limiting date must in each case be the date of the extant manuscripts, and for determining these we have to rely upon internal evidence.

CÆDMON'S HYMN : There are two versions of Cædmon's Hymn which can be dated, the Moore version and the Leningrad one.

Whilst the Moore manuscript is probably the earlier of the two there is on palaeographical grounds less element of doubt in the dating of the Leningrad manuscript. In the first place, the Hymn in the latter manuscript is written in the same eighth-century Anglo-Irish minuscules and by the same hand as the chronological entries at the end (HE Book V. cap. xxiv). Secondly, the different entries in this chronological summary, which themselves give the dates according to the dominical system, are accompanied by marginal roman numbers used to express the dates by a different system. Thus against the first entry *Anno igitur ante incarnationem dominicam sexagesimo Gaius Iulius Cæsar . . . . Brittanias bello pulsauit*, &c., there is a marginal note in the same hand as the text, *ante annos DCCCVI*. This date refers to the entry in the text but is reckoned backwards, so that 806 less the 60 years B.C. would give us A.D. 746 as the year from which the date was reckoned back. So, too, the next entry but one, *Anno incarnationis dominicæ clxvii Eleuther Romæ præsul factus*, &c., is accompanied by the marginal number *DLXXVIIII* ; this number 579 with the dominical year 167 again gives 746. Except in the second entry (where there has been an error of calculation) and excluding those few entries where the marginal figures have been partly cut away by the binder, these marginal dates gradually descend to zero as the dominical number advances, and all uniformly point to the date 746 as the year in which the manuscript was written.[1]

The Moore manuscript presents a somewhat analogous problem. The chronological summary continued from the *Historia Eccles.* (Book V. cap. xxiv) ends with the year 734 at the bottom of fol. 128a, and on the reverse of the folio we have the four lines of Cædmon's Hymn and the ascription of it to Cædmon, the fourth line being filled up by the glosses *arula hearth, destina feurstud, iugulum sticung*, and the words *nota rubrica*.[2] This is followed by a list (in larger writing) of Northumbrian kings down to 737 (but excluding Eadberct who became king that year) and a number of notices of events with the dates of their occurrence reckoned backwards :

Baptizauit Paulinus ante annos CXI.   Eclypsis ante annos LXXIII. Penda moritur ante annos LXXIX.   Pugna Ecgfridi ante annos LXIII.   Ælfuini ante annos LVIII.   Monasterium aet Uuiræmoda ante annos LXIIII.   Cometæ uisæ ante annos VIII.   Eodem anno pater Ecgberct transiuit ad Christum.   Angli in Britanniam ante annos CCXCII.[3]

Zupitza (ZfdA xxii. 215) has shown that not all these entries

[1] For further details cf Olga Dobiache-Rojdestvensky in *Speculum* iii. 316 ff (with plates of the appropriate folios).

[2] *Arula* occurs in HE II. xv, and *destina* in HE III. xvii.

[3] The rest of the page is filled by an extract from Isidore on Consanguinity and prohibited degrees and a decree of Gregory the Great of 721, in a French hand of the tenth century.

agree on one year as the date when they were made ; the third, for instance, would give 734, but the fourth 748 ; but as five of the nine (first, second, fifth, seventh, and eighth) point to the year 737 their consistency easily outweighs the irregularities of the remaining four (which are probably due to errors of calculation), and this date is in agreement with that suggested by the preceding list of Northumbrian kings which terminates at 737.

The question now arises whether the Hymn was written earlier than the list of kings and chronological notices or added later in what would then have been the top margin. Zupitza (*op. cit.* 214) and Sweet (OET 148) think that the hand of the Hymn is not the same as that of the succeeding entries but is coeval with it, but in that case it still remains a possibility, as Sweet says, "that the hymn may have been written later than the list, to fill up the blank space ". But with that one precise limiting date vanishes, for it is really only a short step from Sweet's view that the Hymn is slightly later than the list to the extreme view held by Wülcker (PBB iii. 348 ff) that the Hymn was added by an inexperienced scribe of the eleventh or twelfth century.[1] There are, however, objections to both these views. H. Bradshaw, whilst not stating it explicitly, implied [2] that the *Historia Eccles.*, the Hymn and the remaining matter were all the work of one scribe [3] and there is much in favour of this [4] : apart from the similar shape of the letters and

[1] That a late scribe could carefully imitate an archaic hand is well illustrated by some of the late versions of Bede's Death Song in Symeon of Durham.

[2] Bradshaw (Palaeographical Society, First Series, Vol. II, Part ii. Plate 139) says : " On the succeeding page the scribe closes his work with (1) the original Anglo-Saxon of the Song of Cædmon . . . (2) a list of Northumbrian kings. . . ."

[3] The only difference between the hand of the Hymn and that of the succeeding entries is one of size. None of the scholars who think that we have to deal with different hands has furnished any evidence in support of this view.

[4] If we accept this view, it is necessary to explain why the Hymn is in a smaller hand than the rest. In this the scribe follows the same practice as the scribes who added it in the margins of

the likeness in the general style, the clubbing of the down-strokes is the same, compound letters like *st*, *ae* (*æ*), *en*, &c., are formed in precisely the same way, *a* is always closed at the top, the second downstroke of *r* rarely reaches the bottom line (as in contemporary hands), and in the letter *ʒ* (made in three strokes) and in the usual turned back *d* (*ð*, made in two strokes) the joins of the loops at the bottom right-hand side are frequently badly made, leaving gaps or intersecting ; such a fault as this is very rare in Old English manuscripts (cf F. Norman, *Waldere* Introd.). Taken singly, these characteristics cannot carry much weight, but the cumulative effect favours the view that the *Historia*, the Hymn and the additional entries are the work of one scribe. If this is true, then the Moore version of the Hymn can be definitely assigned to the year 737, which, we have seen, is the date when the additional entries were made.

Yet even if the Hymn is in a different hand it was probably written before the entries which follow and was not added afterwards to fill a blank space. It is unlikely that a margin four or more lines wide would have been left by the scribe of the list of Northumbrian kings, when the preceding pages and the guide lines on the other side of the folio (marked with a stylus) would have shown him the exact place to begin. Nor is it likely that a later scribe adding the Hymn in the top margin would have begun at exactly the same height on this page as the main scribe did on the others and have followed exactly the same line spacing.[1] In this case one can certainly say that this

other MSS of the HE, where it is generally in a smaller hand. After allowing for generous cuttings by binders, the margins of the Moore MS could hardly have been wide enough to allow of the insertion of the Hymn at the usual place (opposite Book IV, cap. xxiv). The scribe therefore added it at the first available place in the MS, that is, at the beginning of fol. 128b. He then continued the remaining entries in the more usual size of writing. The use of this smaller writing for the Hymn would be analogous to the use of small type in a modern work to isolate matter which is illustrative but not essential to the principal argument.

[1] Cf A. Schroer in *Archiv* cxv. 67–8.

version of Cædmon's Hymn was written after 734 (the date of the last entry recorded on folio 128a and therefore the earliest date at which that part of the manuscript could have been completed) and in or before 737, the date when the list of Northumbrian kings and the chronological entries were made. At the outside, therefore, the two earliest versions of the Hymn represent the state of the language at the end of the seventh or beginning of the eighth century.

BEDE'S DEATH SONG and the LEIDEN RIDDLE : Beyond the palaeographical evidence there is nothing to indicate the date of the extant versions of Bede's Death Song and the Leiden Riddle. Both are written in Carolingian minuscules and both belong to the ninth century. The Leiden Riddle is probably the older manuscript, for in it there is a remnant of an older script in the frequent use of the open *a* ; both bows of *ʒ* are open, shaped like a 3, the heads of the long downstrokes are clubbed and there are few traces of serifs. On the other hand, in the manuscript of Bede's Death Song the open *a* is not used, the top loop of the *g* is closed and there are frequent examples of an oblique serif at the head of long downstrokes ; it is on the whole a very late ninth-century hand. There is thus no independent evidence to show as precisely as in the case of Cædmon's Hymn to what period the language of these two poems can be assigned.

LOCALIZATION OF THE TEXTS : The original dialect of Cædmon's Hymn and Bede's Death Song was certainly Northumbrian, but that of the Leiden Riddle we do not know (cf *supra* p. 18). As to the provenance of the extant versions of the three poems we cannot speak with absolute certainty. The Leiden Riddle and Bede's Death Song were written on the Continent and, judging by the character of the handwriting, somewhere within the Frankish Empire.[1] The Leningrad manuscript of Cædmon's Hymn,

[1] The MS of Bede's Death Song may have been written at St Gall, where, like many other MSS written there in the ninth century, it is still preserved ; the hand is not unlike those of other MSS written

3   23

with its characteristic Anglo-Irish pointed minuscules, may have been written in England, probably the north, whilst the Moore manuscript was probably transcribed at some English colony in the north of France.[1] Thus three of the earliest specimens of English literature that we have are preserved in continental manuscripts, and we owe their preservation largely to the influence exerted on the Continent by the great English missionaries like Willibrord and Boniface and to scholars like Alcuin of York. There is good evidence about the way in which such works arrived there, for throughout the eighth century these English missionaries repeatedly begged the gift of books *ad consolationem peregrinationis*. Thus, about 735 Boniface sent a letter of thanks to Eadburg, abbess of Thanet, for *sanctorum librorum munera*, and about the same time he asked Nothelm, Archbishop of Canterbury, to send him *Augustini Interrogationes et Gregorii responsiones*.[2] Some ten years later he asked Ecgbert, Archbishop of York, to send him copies of Bede's works and sent a similar request to Huetberht, abbot of Wearmouth and Jarrow.[3] In 764 Cuthbert, abbot of the same monastery, sent Lullus, Boniface's successor, copies of Bede's *Lives of St. Cuthbert* and apologized for not having sent all the works of Bede that Lullus required, as the work of transcription at Jarrow had been retarded *quia presentia preteriti hiemis multum horribiliter insulam nostrae gentis in frigore et gelu et ventorum et imbrium procellis diu lateque depressit*.[4] The works of Bede were in the greatest demand, but between 732 and 740 we find Lullus asking Dealwin to send him copies of the works of Aldhelm.[5] That copies of such

in that great scriptorium (cf for example, the Book of Canons, Plate 186, Pal. Soc., First Series, Vol. II. Part 2).

[1] Thus the gatherings are marked by *Q* (with a number), a practice usual in the north of France but not in England. Cf further H. Bradshaw, *op. cit.*, Plate 139.

[2] MGH, Epistolae: Karol. Aevum I. 281, 283.

[3] Ib. 347, 348 ; Ecgbert was a friend of Bede's (cf *supra* p. 16) ; Huetberht was abbot at the time of Bede's death.

[4] Ib. 405.   [5] Ib. 338.

works were made on the Continent is certain. Thus at the important scriptorium at Tours copies were made of Bede's works,[1] and in 801 Alcuin wrote to Gisla, abbess of Chelles, sending Bede's works to be transcribed for him.[2] Whether the works with which we are concerned were transcribed by Englishmen on the Continent is not known, but it is reasonable to suppose that the Moore manuscript was, for its handwriting is of an insular type and the three Old English glosses were probably added by the scribe of this manuscript.[3] In the Leiden manuscript the uncial letters sometimes have dotted surrounds, following an English type of ornamentation, and the English glosses after the list of Aldhelm's riddles might also possibly suggest an English scribe.[4] But there is nothing to show that an English scribe copied the Death Song. At the same time, if they are the work of foreigners unfamiliar with English, they are clearly faithful copies, Cædmon's Hymn and Bede's Death Song of early Northumbrian originals and the Leiden Riddle possibly so.

For such reasons, therefore, neither Bede's Death Song (735–end of the ninth century) nor the Leiden Riddle (c. 695 to ninth century) can be used as evidence of the state of English at a given date, nor can we safely use the Leiden Riddle as evidence of the Northumbrian dialect : the date when these two texts assumed their present form

[1] Plummer's *Bede* I. xx note.

[2] MGH, Epistolae : Karol. Aevum II. 360.

[3] Schroer in *Archiv* cxv. 69 considers that the scribe of M copied the Hymn from a MS which already contained the glosses ; that the scribe was copying another MS is clear from its textual closeness to L, but L lacks the glosses, as would any MS which has the Hymn in the margin of Book IV. cap. xxiv (which was certainly the usual place for it).

[4] These glosses are not found in any other MS of Aldhelm's riddles (cf *supra* p. 7 note 4). But the fact that they form part of a later glossary and have nothing to do with either the riddles of Symphosius or those of Aldhelm makes it likely that they were simply added here from another MS. On the possibility of the scribe being a slavish copier of his original for the Riddle cf *supra* p. 8. These points however prove nothing, one way or the other.

and the dialect of the extant version of the Riddle can only be determined by comparing them linguistically with such a text as Cædmon's Hymn, which can, with some degree of accuracy, be independently dated and localized.

IV. ORTHOGRAPHY AND LANGUAGE

1. ORTHOGRAPHY. The orthography of these texts is for the most part based on the Latin alphabet introduced with Christianity in the seventh century; it was in the process of being adapted to the recording of the vernacular, and this fact should be borne in mind. Of the various symbols in use in Old English CH(M) has both *ae* (6) and *æ* (5), (DP) having *ae* only and (L) only *æ*; BDS has *ae* only and LR has both *ae* (14), *æ* (8) and the mediæval Latin symbol *ę* (1). The runic letters *þ* and *p* have not yet been borrowed; the former is represented in CH(M) by *th* and *d* (*ʒidanc*), in CH(L) and BDS by *th*, and in LR by *th* (5) and *ð* (15), a symbol found as early as 742 (OET 432). *w* (*p*) is represented by *u* in all texts (*uerc, huaet, uarp*), but BDS also has *uu* (*uueorthae*) and the prototype of CH (D and P) had *p* initially (cf *puldur, peard*) and *u* medially (*suae, gihuaes*). A characteristic of the early orthography of this type is the use of the letters *c* (before *t*), *d* and *b* to represent the fricatives [χ], [ð] and [v] or [ƀ]: *d* has been mentioned *supra* (in CH.M). CH(M) has *ct* (*maecti, dryctin*), CH(L) has *ct* and *ht* (*dryctin, mehti*), LR has *ht* (*hyhtlic* and, by error, *biuorthæ*); *b* is found once in CH(M) in *heben* (also *hefaen-*) and twice in LR *ob* (but *ofaer*).[1] The orthography of LR in the use of *ht* for *c(h)t* and *ð* for *th* would appear to be later than that of the other texts, for in the *Liber Vitae Dunelmensis th* is still very common and *ct* or *cht* is the regular form, and *b* for *f* was still in use (cf Müller 27).

---

[1] The variation between such forms is due to the difficulty experienced by the earliest writers of OE in adapting the symbols of one language to represent those of another, especially when certain sounds (and consequently symbols for them) did not exist in the former.

2. In BDS *uuiurthit* (*-t* for *-th*) and LR *ðret* (for *ðred*) there is the possibility of the influence of Frankish scribes (cf *anoeȝun* § 18 note), though the former may be a Nb scribal form (like *fallet*, &c., cf Lindelöf 207). BDS *deoth-* (for *death-*) may show a trace of the older spelling for PrOE *ǣo* (WGerm *au*) and BDS *neid-* is probably a Nb spelling for *nēd-* (Bülbring § 505 note) or it may possibly represent an early stage in the *i*-mutation of *ēa* (cf M. Förster, ESt lvi. 220) ; in BDS *aeththa* (cf Nb *eðða*) *ae* is due to the influence of Latin orthography (cf § 9c *infra*). LR *ȝoelu* is clearly an error for *ȝeolu*.

3. FEATURES DUE TO ORIGINAL GERMANIC DIFFERENCES. Some forms (characteristic of the early language or of the Nb dialect) are derived from Germanic forms that differed from the commonly used ones. Thus, CH(M) *end* (cf OHG *enti*, OSax *endi*, &c.) is from PrGerm **andi* whilst CH(LDP) *and* (cf OFris *ande*) is from PrGerm **anda*. So too BDS *aeththa* (cf Goth *aíþþau*, OSax *eððo*, OHG *eddo*) and the more common *oððe* (cf OSax *oððe*, OHG *odho*), and *ðer(i)h* (cf Goth *þairh*) with *þurh* (cf OSax *thurh*, OHG *durh*, *duruh*). LR *mith* by the side of *mid* is from a form unaffected by the operation of Verner's Law (PrGerm **miþi*, **miði*), and with CH *fadur* by the side of the more common *fæder* we may compare the OScand *fǫður* (PrGerm **faðurz* by the side of **faðraz*). CH, LR *sue* is from **swā*, a WGerm lengthened form of **swa* which by OE lengthening normally became *swā* (on LR *suae* cf § 6 note). CH(ML) *astelidæ* (for the normal unmutated CH(DP) *astalde*, which like other weak verbs of class Ib formed its past tense with *-dæ*) is from a pa.t. in *-idæ* (with *i*-mutation). In CH *foldu*, CH(DP), LR *eorðu*, the acc. sg. of fem. *n*-stems is regularly derived from PrOE *-un* (PrGerm *-ōnum*, cf van Helten, PBB xv. 461, xxi. 462, xxxvi. 480, and Carpenter § 415), whilst the more usual *-an* forms are analogical from other oblique cases (gen., dat.) ; cf § 18a.

(a) *end* (*aend* Epinal 98) is confined to the seventh, eighth and early ninth centuries (Erfurt, Corpus, Franks Casket, and charters up to 836 OET 47. 10). It is commonest in Angl documents, but even there it is rare; its occurrence in a Kt charter (OET 40. 8) makes it an unreliable test for dialect.

(b) *aeththa* (*eðða*) is still rarer and is, apart from one instance in Exeter Book riddles (43. 16), found only in Nb.

(c) *ðer(i)h* (*ðærh*) is also rare and is confined to Nb (cf NED s.v. *through*, and Anglia xxxiv. 497).

(d) *mið* in later OE is confined to Nb (cf Miller I. xlviii), but in early OE it had a wider provenance (Epinal 796, Corpus 1591, Bede Glosses 70, Merc charter in OET 48. 3). As in other cases its non-occurrence in WSax is due to the paucity of early texts from that area.

(e) *fadur* (*feadur* in Vespas. Psalt. 44. 11, Mercian Hymns 12. 4, &c.) occurs only in Anglian dialects.

(f) *-u* inflexion in *n*-stems is confined to Nb (cf Girvan § 285, note 1).

4. PHONOLOGICAL CHARACTERISTICS. In the following paragraphs no attempt is made to deal with the history of the sounds as a whole; only such forms are dealt with as may throw some light upon the date and place of origin of the extant texts principally by comparison with other early OE texts which can be dated on other than purely linguistic grounds, such as charters, glosses, the proper names in Bede's HE (various MSS), the LVD, and the Nb Gospels.

5. WGerm *a* before a nasal (+ consonant) appears as *a* and *o* in the same texts: CH *ʒidanc* (M), *-thanc* (L), *-d(e)anc* (DP), *and* (LDP), *mon* (MLDP); BDS *than*, *thonc*, *hiniongae*; LR *ouana*, *uonʒ*,

(a) In the oldest texts (such as Epinal, charters as 692–3 *angen-labeshaam*, OET 426) it appears as *a* (Bülbring, § 123), but from a very early date *o* is also used, as HE(M) *tilmon*, charter 759 *onnanduun*, &c. (OET 430); in LVD *o* is usual, *a* being found only twice (Müller 1, 2). In later Nb texts *o* is regular (Lindelöf, § 44).

(b) *hiniongae* (later *ʒeonʒ*, for WSax *gang*, *gong*) is a Nb form (cf. NED s.v. *yong*, and Bülbring § 492 note 1; Girvan § 227).

6. WGerm *ā* appears as *ē*: CH(ML) *sue* (§ 3); LR *ueta*, *herum*, *ðret*. Angl *ǣ* from smoothing of WGerm *au* (§ 11) also became *ē*: LR *heh*, *ðeh*.

WGerm $\bar{a}$ appears as $\bar{æ}$ in WSax but $\bar{e}$ in other dialects (Luick § 117) ; *ae* (*æ*) appears sporadically in some Nb texts as HE (M) *Suæbhardo* (king of Wessex), *Raedfridum*, where *æ* may be due to Bede citing the form in his source, at any rate in the case of *Suæbhardo* ; but in HE (M) as in LVD (Müller 10) and the later Nb texts (Lindelöf § 26) *e* is the usual form. For this reason it is probable that LR and CH(DP) *suae* had a short vowel (as in Ritual and Lindisf. *svæ, suæ*) and this probably represents the regular OE development of WGerm *a* (which may have remained unlengthened in unstressed positions).

7. WGerm *eu* and *iu*. PrGerm *eu* normally becomes OE *ēo* : LR *freoriʒ* ; in WGerm it became *iu* when *i/j* followed in the next syllable and *iu* remains in the earliest documents, later Angl *īo*, WSax *ēo* (WSax *īe, ȳ* by *i*-mutation) : LR *fliusum, niudlicae*.

iu is written in early texts : *sniuuith* Epinal 669, *piustra* Corpus 152 (cf Dieter, *Über Sprache und Mundart der ältesten englischen Denkmäler* § 26), and once in LVD in *Liutfrith* (Müller 15), but it was also written *io* in the earliest records (as *briosa*, Epinal 27) ; *io* is common in LVD and is regular in later Nb (Lindelöf §§ 40, 41) ; in WSax it usually underwent *i*-mutation to *īe*, later *ȳ* (as *flȳsum*). Only in Nb were WGerm *eu* and *iu* kept apart (cf Bülbring § 111) ; for this reason LR is Nb and it may belong to any period up to about LVD or slightly later.

8. Breaking : (*a*) WGerm *a* before *r* + consonant remains mostly unbroken : CH (ML) *uard* (twice), *barnum* (L) *ʒard*, but (M) *ʒeard* ; (DP) only broken forms : *p(u)eard, bearnum, geard* ; BDS *tharf* ; LR *uarp, aeriʒ*.

HE(M) has broken and unbroken forms (*beardaneu, peartaneu, Farne, barue*) ; LVD has mostly broken forms as *bearnhard, badheard* (Müller 2–3). In other Angl texts there is also fluctuation between broken and unbroken forms (cf Bülbring § 132).

(*b*) WGerm *e* before *r* + consonant is *eo* : CH(DP) *eordu*, LR *eorðu*, BDS *uueorthae*.

This was the common OE development ; on CH *uerc*, LR *ðerh, ðerih*, cf § 11.

(*c*) WGerm *i* before *r* + consonant is normally broken to *iu* (preserved sporadically in forms like LVD *Iurminburg*), later Nb *io*, Merc, WSax *eo*, but the combination *wir* + consonant appears to have become *wyr-* (cf Luick § 155 note 2) : BDS *uuiurthit*.

M. Förster (*Lesebuch* 64) suggests that *iu* in BDS is due to Continental influence and represents OE *y*; *ui* was certainly a symbol for *y* (as in HE *Thruidred* = *Thrydred*, Corpus *gruiit* = *gryt*, cf Girvan § 79 note 2), and perhaps *iu* is an error for *ui* which would be avoided in an unusual form like **uuuirthit*, though there is no reason why *iu* should not itself be a symbol for *y*; a parallel is possibly found in *sciulun* (§ 13b).

(*d*) WGerm *a* before *l* + consonant was unbroken : CH(DP) *astalde*; on CH(ML) *aelda* cf § 9a(iv), and on *astelidæ* cf §§ 3, 9.

WGerm *a* was unbroken before *l* + consonant in Angl dialects, and unbroken forms are found occasionally in the earliest Saxon and Kt charters (e.g. *ualdharius* 693–731 OET 427, *aldhodi* 679 ib. 428, etc), but these are conventional spellings of proper names (cf Girvan § 62 note 1).

(*e*) WGerm *a* before *h* + consonant was broken, but the effects of breaking were obscured by smoothing and *i*-mutation; cf §§ 9a, 11b.

9. *i*-mutation : (*a*) WGerm *a* (PrOE *æ*) became *e* (i) before single consonants : CH *herʒa(n)*, *astelidæ* (cf § 3), *eci*; (ii) after PrOE *æ* was broken to *æo* (before *h* + consonant) : CH *allmectiʒ*, (LDP) *me(c)hti* (this being non-WSax, Bülbring § 180); (iii) after diphthongization after palatals (whereby *a* had become *ea*, cf § 13) : CH(M) *scepen*, (LDP) *sceppend* (non-WSax, cf Bülbring §§ 168 note 2, 182); (iv) it became *æ* before *l* + consonant when unbroken in Angl (Bülbring § 175, Girvan § 74d) : CH(ML) *aelda*; (v) before nasals it became *æ*, later raised to *e* : LR *cændæ*, CH(M) *end* (cf § 3), and also in medial syllables as LR *hrutendu* and the gerund in *-enne* (though in BDS *-hycggannae* has been influenced by the infinitive).

(1) *æ* before a nasal is preserved in the oldest texts as *ænid* Epinal 17, *aend* ib 98, *anhaendi* Erfurt 626, &c; HE(M) has *Rendil*, but the late eighth-century MS Tiberius C II has *Raendil*; but it is generally uncommon in the eighth century, having already been

raised to *e* (Bülbring § 170), which is also found in the earliest texts (Erfurt, Corpus, HE, &c.) ; LVD (except for *Kaenta*) and the later Nb texts have *e* (Müller 4, 5, Lindelöf § 70) ; the odd form in LR might therefore be as late in date as LVD.

(2) In LR *hęliðum* we may have an instance of secondary mutation (cf Luick § 198).

(*b*) PrOE *u* is normally mutated to *y* : CH(ML) *dryctin*, *moncynnæs*, BDS *ymbhycggannae*, LR *hyʒiðoncum*, *cnyssa*, *hyhtlic*. This *y* has had further developments (cf § 13b).

(*c*) WGerm *ai* (PrOE *ā*) became *æ* : CH *aerist*, BDS *aer*, *naenig*, LR *aerest*.

(1) *æ* was regular in Anglian and WSax, Kt having *ē* (Bülbring § 167).

(2) BDS *them* for the more regular *thaem* (suggested by *thae* in MS B) is probably only a scribal variant with *e* for *ae* as is frequent in Latin orthography of the time ; cf also *gastae* in MSS AB, *gaste* in EIL, *uueorthae* in A, *uueorthe* in I, *się* in I but *sie* in AB, &c., and on *aeththa* cf § 2.

(*d*) WGerm *o* became *oe* : BDS *doemid*, LR *anoeʒun*.

oe was common in all dialects in the eighth century and remained in later Nb ; *e* forms appear in the eighth century (cf Bülbring §§ 164–5) ; about a quarter of the examples in LVD have *e* (Müller 12).

(*e*) WGerm *au* was mutated in Angl and Kt to *ē* : BDS *neid-* (cf § 2).

(*f*) In three cases *i*-mutation has not taken place : CH(M) *maecti* (cf a(ii) *supra*), and LR *fliusum*, *niud-* (cf § 7).

10. Back-mutation. There is no back-mutation of *i* : CH(L) *scilun*, LR *innaðae* ; *e* is generally unaffected as CH *metudæs*, (DP) *hefun*, but is mutated in LR *ʒeolu* (MS *ʒoelu*) (cf Girvan §§ 102, 107).

In the oldest texts there is little evidence of back-mutation except in Corpus (cf Luick § § 224 note 4, 228 note 5). HE(M) has unmutated forms (*Heruteu*, &c.) though the later MS Tiberius C II has *eo* (*Heorutford*) ; LVD has *e* (once) and *eo* (twice), but unmutated *i* is more frequent than *io* (Müller 6, 8). In later Nb texts *eo* (from *e*) and *io* (from *i*) are regular (Lindelöf §§ 83–6) ; on mutation before *nn* in Nb cf Bülbring § 249. From this it would appear that CH is earlier than LVD, and LR might be as late, but the evidence is inadequate.

11. Smoothing of diphthongs in Anglian (cf Luick §§ 235 ff) :

(*a*) WGerm diphthongs : *au* (PrOE *ǣo*) was smoothed to *ǣ* (later *ē*, cf § 6) : LR *heh, ðeh*.

(*b*) Diphthongs from breaking : PrOE *æo* (WGerm *a*) becomes *ae* (without *i*-mutation, cf § 9f) : CH(M) *maecti* ; PrOE *eo* (WGerm *e*) becomes *e* : CH *uerc*, LR *ðerh, ðerih* ; PrOE *iu* (WGerm *i*) becomes *i* (later *ī* with loss of χ, cf § 15) : CH *tiadæ, tiade*.

12. Development of a paragogic vowel between *r* and a following back or front consonant: LR *ðerih* (also *ðerh*), *aeriȝ*.

HE has *Cyniberict* (also *Cyniberct*), LVD has *Berecht* (also *Bercht*) ; cf Girvan § 181.

Before ȝ there was no paragogic vowel: CH *herȝa(n)*.

This development was confined to WSax (Girvan § 182); in later Nb forms like *sveriga* are formed by analogy with weak verbs of class II (Bülbring § 451).

13. Influence of palatal consonants:

(*a*) after initial palatals *sc-* and *ȝ-*, WGerm *a* appears as *ea*: LR *sceal, ȝeatum*; on *sceppend* cf § 9a.

Such forms are usual in WSax and Northern Nb (cf Girvan § 65 and Bülbring § 155 and note).

(*b*) In Nb PrOE *sku-* became *sciu-* (cf CH(DP) *sciulun*, with initial palatal by analogy from *sceal*, &c.), which became *scy-* (cf CH(M) *scylun*) ; cf E. Sievers, *Zum ags. Vokalismus* § 27. 3 and Luick § 170 note) ; under the influence of palatals *y* is unrounded to *i*: CH(L) *scilun* ; cf also CH(DP) *drichtin* ; *monncinnes* (by an analogy with forms like *cining* for *cyning*).

(*a*) It is of course possible that *sciulun* in CH(DP), which Wuest read as *scuilun*, should be interpreted as *scylun*, as in CH(M); cf *uuiurthit* § 8c.

(*b*) Unrounding after palatals is rare and is confined to WSax and later Nb, but CH(L) shows that it could be found as early as 746. Before palatals it is common in late WSax, frequent in later Nb, but rare in Kt (Bülbring §§ 307, 308).

14. Loss of final -*n* in oblique cases of *n*-stems, in the infinitive and in some adverbs occurs in the earliest texts (CH) and is commoner in later Nb (cf Bülbring § 557) ; CH *foldu*, CH(LDP) *herga*, (DP) *eordu*, but CH(M) *herȝan* ; LR *eorðu, cnyssa, ouana*, but *uullan, hatan*. It is not lost in the pret. or pret.-pres. plur. : CH *scylun*, LR *auefun*.

15. Contraction of vowels and palatal consonants : *i* + palatal and back vowel appears as *īa* : CH *tiade* from *tihodæ (cf § 11b) with Nb -*adæ* for -*odæ* (cf Kolbe § 170 and also Girvan § 112) ; LR *biað* from PrGerm *bijanþi which became *bī-ōþ*, with *bīað* in Nb (as in Ritual, Lindisf.) by analogy with 3 pres. pl. of strong verbs (Bülbring § 118 note 5).

16. VOWELS OF THE UNSTRESSED SYLLABLES : PrOE *æ*, later *e*.

(*a*) Case endings : PrGerm -*aso* (g.sg. *a*-, *ja*-stems) : CH -*ricaes, -æs, metudæs* (in MLDP), -*cynnæs* (ML) but -*cinnes* (DP), BDS *godaes, yflaes* ; PrGerm -*ai* (dat.sg. *a*-, *ja*-, *ō*-stems) : CH(L) *hrofæ* but (MDP) *hrofe*, BDS *faerae, hiniongae, gastae, hycggannae*, but *daege, fore* (adv. *furai) (cf also § 9c note), LR *innaðae* and adv. forms *huethrae, uidæ, niudlicae* ; PrGerm -*ai* (nom. pl. adj. p.pt.) LR *uundnae* ; PrGerm -*ōz* (nom.pl. *ō*-stems, cf Flasdieck, IF xlviii, pp. 53–66) LR *ueflæ* ; PrGerm -*ōn* (fem.acc.sg. *ō*-stems and adj., p.pt.) LR *faerae, biuorthæ*.

(*b*) Suffixes : PrGerm -*ag*- : CH(M) *haleȝ* ; PrGerm -*en*(*oz*) : CH(M) *hefaen*, but also CH(M) *heben*, (L) *hefen*, (DP) *efen* ; PrGerm -*er* : LR *ofaer*, but CH, BDS *aefter*.

OE -*ig* in *freoriȝ* LR, *haliȝ* CH may be analogical (with forms like *naenig* from PrGerm -*ig*- § 17b which have *i*-mutation), but it is also possible that PrGerm -*ag*- which had become -*eȝ* was further raised to -*ig* through the influence of the palatal -*ȝ* (cf Luick § 327). On CH(DP) *hefun* cf Girvan § 166 note 2, and on PrOE -*æn* from PrGerm -*enoz*, &c., and -*aer* from -*er* cf Bülbring § 369. 1.

(c) Verbal endings: PrGerm -*ǣ*(*þ*) (3sg.pa.t. w.vs):
CH(ML) *astelidæ, tiadæ* but (DP) *astalde, tiade*, LR (?)
cændæ ; PrGerm -*ai* (3sg.pr.subj.) : BDS *uueorthae* but
sie (cf § 9c note).

LR *hafæ* is a rare form and may have been influenced by (if it
is not actually itself) the 1sg.pres.subj. (PrGerm -*jai*) ; the normal
Nb 1sg.pres.ind. is *hafu, hafo* (cf Kolbe § 197).

LR has *æ* uniformly (10), CH(ML) more *æ* than *e* (6*æ*, 3*e*), BDS
also has more *æ* than *e* forms (7*æ*, 5*e*), whilst CH(DP) have more *e*
forms (2*æ*, 7*e*). In the oldest texts *æ* (*ae*) is usual but occasional
e forms are found (cf Sievers, PBB viii. 324), as charters 692–3
uuidmundes- (OET 426), 700–15 *pleghelmes*-, *meguuines*- (ib. 428),
&c., in HE(M) *hefenfeld, cnobheresburg, clofeshoh*, &c., and in HE
(Tiberius MS C II) *e* is still commoner (*uilfaresdun*, &c.). In LVD
both *æ* and *e* occur, *æ* being commoner (cf Müller 22), but Lindisf.
and other later Nb texts have *e* regularly (cf Carpenter §§ 62 ff,
Lindelöf §§ 115–16). If any weight can be attached to these forms
in the texts it would appear that none of them is as late as Lindisf.,
that LR is as old if not older than CH(ML), and that CH(DP) are
rather later than LVD. Such conclusions, however, are rather
dubious as we are dealing here with letters, not sounds, and it is not
possible to estimate how far *ae* (*æ*) may be an orthographic fossil.
The problem may also depend partly upon the habit of a scribe
when writing Latin -*ae* as -*ae*, -*æ*, -*ę* or -*e* (cf § 9c note). The most
one can safely say is that BDS and LR might have been written
anywhere in the seventh, eighth or ninth centuries and CH(DP)
rather in the later part of this period.

17. Unstressed PrOE *i*, later *e*.

(a) Case endings : PrGerm -*ijiz* (original n.pl. *i*-stems) :
CH(M) *maecti*, (LDP) *me*(*c*)*hti* (acc.pl.) ; PrGerm -*iz*
(n.sg. *i*-stems, after short syllables) : LR *hyʒi*- ; PrGerm
-*jaz* (n.sg. *ja*-stems, after short syllables) : CH *eci* (from
*ajukjaz).

LR *uyrdi* is fem.gen.sg. for -*e* (Exeter Book has *wyrda* gen.pl.) ;
the origin of -*i* is uncertain ; it may be from PrGerm -*īz* from IE
-*eis* beside masc.gen.sg. -*aiz* (IE -*ois*) or it may be simply formed on
the analogy of the dat.sg. (PrGerm -*ī*) ; cf Girvan § 279, Streitberg,
Urgerm. Grammatik 242.

(b) Suffixes : PrGerm -*inaz* : CH *dryctin, drichtin* ;
PrGerm -*ist*- : CH(ML) *aerist* (but LR *aerest*) ; PrGerm
-*iʒaz* : CH *allmec*(*h*)*tiʒ*, BDS *naenig* (cf also § 16b).

(c) Verbal endings: PrGerm *-iþi* (3sg.pres.ind. strong verbs): BDS *uuiurthit*, LR *hlimmith*; PrGerm *-ið-* (3sg.pa.t. weak verbs): CH(ML) *astelidæ* (on *astalde* cf § 3); PrGerm *-iðaz* (p.pt.): BDS *doemid*.

(d) Particles: PrGerm *ʒi*: CH(ML) *ʒidanc, ʒithanc* but (DP) *ged(e)anc*, CH(MLDP) *ʒihuaes*, LR *ʒiðraec, ʒiuæde*; WGerm *ni*: LR *ni* (6), *ne* (1); WGerm *þi*: LR *ði* (2).

In the oldest texts *i* is the usual spelling, but an occasional *e* is found (as in charters 692–3 *oedelraedus* OET 426, 742; *æðelbaldi, -berhti, hereuald, cyneberht* ib. 432, 770; *cyneðryð* ib. 431, &c.); in the proper names in HE(M) *i* is usual but an occasional *e* is found as in *hererici, hereberct*; *e* is more common in the late eighth-century MS Tiberius C II (*haengest, uulfhere, cynemund*, &c., OET 132 ff), and in LVD (*Dene-, Here-*, cf Müller 21); *i* remains in later Nb texts but to a much smaller extent (cf Lindelöf § 101).

CH(ML) have no *e* forms, nor has BDS; CH(DP) have one *e* (five in *i*) and LR has 2 *e* (12 *i*, including *ni* 6). The only probable conclusion is that LR and CH(DP) are later than CH(ML) and BDS and may be as late as the ninth century, though the isolated *e* forms have not much weight in view of the early occurrence of *e* in other texts.

18. Unstressed PrOE *u*, later *o, a*.

(a) Case endings: PrGerm *-ōnum* (WGerm *-ūnum*) became *-un*, later *-u* (acc.sg.fem. *n*-stems, cf also § 14) CH *foldu*, (DP) *eordu*, LR *eorðu*.

Gen.sg. of *n*-stems normally ends in *-an*, masc. PrGerm *-onez* (WGerm *-aniz*) as LR *eʒsan*, fem. PrGerm *-ōnez* (WGerm *-ōniz*) as LR *uullan*. CH(DP) *eordu*, if it is gen.sg., is therefore an analogical form, unless it was wrongly taken as acc. object after *scoop*. This *-u* inflexion is characteristic of Nb. In later Nb *eorðu* (nom. sg.) was indeclinable; on the paradigm of this word *v.* Alan S. C. Ross's forthcoming *Studies in the Accidence of the Lindisfarne Gospels*.

(b) Suffixes: PrGerm *-ur(az)*: CH *uuldur*; PrGerm *-juma-, -jun-* CH(MDP) *middun-*, but (L) *middin-*; cf also *fadur* (§ 3) and (DP) *hefun* (arising out of an old syncopated form, Girvan § 166 and notes).

(c) Verbal endings: PrGerm *-un* (3pl.pa.t.ind.) CH *scylun*, &c., LR *auefun*.

LR *ðreatun* (cf Exeter Book *þreata* gen.pl.) and *anoeʒun* (1sg.

35

pres.indic. = Lat *uereor*) are obscure. Schlutter gets over the difficulty of the former by reading *ðreaunȝiðraec* and by taking this as a compound *ðreaunȝ-ȝiðraec* (cf LR note to line 6), and for the latter he proposes *anoeȝnu*, which is not an impossible form from a verb *anoegnan* (cf examples of the ending *-u*, *-o* in Kolbe § 197) ; the distinction between *n* and *u* is clear in the MS, so that if Schlutter's correction is right then there must have been confusion between *n* and *u* in the prototype, but in the Anglo-Irish minuscule and in the early Carolingian hands *n* and *u* were generally distinguishable. In the case of *anoeȝun*, however, there is the possibility of a Continental form due to a Frankish scribe who associated the verb with OHG *egisôn* 'to dread', which would have the 1sg.pres.ind. in *-on*, *-un* (of Braune, *Althochdeutsche Grammatik* § 305). At the same time the original reading may have been *anoeȝa* (for the ending cf Kolbe *l.c.*), and the most satisfactory explanation would cover both this and *ðreatun* (? for *ðreata*) : the scribe of the Leiden MS never uses a round *a*, and it is possible that if his prototype were in the Anglo-Irish minuscule he misread a round *a* as *u* with a nasal mark over it. (See further p. 47, n. 13.)

In the earliest texts PrOE *u* generally remained, but *o* is found occasionally as in Corpus *eofor*, HE(M) *earconuald* ; in the late eighth-century MS Tiberius C II *u* is almost invariable and *u* is the prevailing form in LVD though here *o* also occurs a number of times (Müller 21). In later Nb texts *o* is the regular form, but *u* is still occasionally found (Lindelöf § 101). As CH, BDS and LR have only *u*, these texts may antedate LVD where *o* begins to appear more frequently.

19. DIALECT. On grounds already stated, Cædmon's Hymn (MSS M and L) is *a priori* Northumbrian and a comparative examination of the material in the foregoing paragraphs shows that Bede's Death Song and the Leiden Riddle are also written in the same dialect.

Certain features are definitely Nb, and there is supporting evidence in features which are Anglian, non-WSax and non-Kt :

Cædmon's Hymn (ML) : Nb §§ 14, 15, 18a ; Angl §§ 3d, 8a, 9a (iv), 11 ; non-Kt § 9c ; non-WSax §§ 9a(ii), 9a(iii), 12.

Cædmon's Hymn (DP) : Nb §§ 14, 15, 18a ; Angl §§ 3d, 8d, 11 ; non-Kt §§ 9c, 13 ; non-WSax §§ (?6), 9a(ii), 9a(iii), 12.

Bede's Death Song (cf *supra* p. 25) : Nb §§ 3b, 5b, 9e (cf § 2) ; Angl § 8a ; non-Kt § 9c ; non-WSax § 9e.

Leiden Riddle : Nb §§ 3c, 7, 14, 15, 18a ; Angl §§ 8a, 11 ; non-Kt § 9c ; non-WSax § 6.

20. DATE. In some of the forms mentioned in this section it would appear that in the earliest stages of the written language scribal practices varied in different dialects, so that a fair comparison between Cædmon's Hymn, &c., and other early and non-Nb texts is not quite possible (cf for instance §§ 16, 17). On the whole the Nb orthography tends to be rather more archaic than that of other dialects. Further, certain later features are found in very early texts (cf §§ 16, 17) and other early features are preserved in later texts (cf § 9a, v). There is not enough evidence to determine the habits of individual scribes, so that statistical comparisons can have little reliability. The two versions of Cædmon's Hymn (M and L), which were written down within a dozen years of each other, agree very closely (cf §§ 3, 5, 16, 17) and the language of these two versions is rather more archaic than the rest of the texts ; if anything, the language of M is a little older than L (cf §§ 1, 8e, 9b, 13b, 14)   Besides this, it is probable that Bede's Death Song is the oldest of the three non-dated texts : it is earlier than LVD (early ninth century) and possibly earlier than the DP version of Cædmon's Hymn and the Leiden Riddle (cf §§ 5, 17) ; it might be contemporary with Cædmon's Hymn (ML) or a little later : in other words it may represent Cuthbert's copy of the Song very faithfully. The Leiden Riddle is also earlier than LVD (§§ 5, 9a(v), 18b, c, and possibly 7) ; it is later than Cædmon's Hymn (ML) and probably Bede's Death Song (§§ 1, 17) ; it may belong to the middle or second half of the eighth century, though in one feature (§ 16) it may be as old as MSS M and L of Cædmon's Hymn. The versions D and P of Cædmon's Hymn are later than the ML versions (§§ 13, 17), perhaps a little later than Bede's Death Song and the Leiden Riddle (§ 16), and earlier than LVD (§§ 5, 10, 18b, c) ; the language of their original (*Y) may belong to the second half of the eighth century.

CÆDMON'S HYMN

Northumbrian Version

(MS Cambridge University Library Kk, 5. 16)

Nu scylun herȝan   hefaenricaes uard,
metudæs maecti   end his modȝidanc,
3   uerc uuldurfadur   sue he uundra ȝihuaes,
eci dryctin,   or astelidæ ;
he aerist scop   aelda barnum
6   heben til hrofe,   haleȝ scepen,

VARIANT READINGS : (1) *nu* : DP *nupue* ; *scylun* : L *scilun*, DP *sciulun* (*pene* A. S. C. Ross, *scuilun* Wuest) ; *herȝan* : M *herȝen* with *e* dotted for deletion and *a* written above the line, L *herȝa*, DP *herga* ; *hefaen* : L *hefen*, DP *hefun* ; *ricaes* : L *ricæs*, P *rinca es* ; *uard* : DP *pueard*.

(2) *metudæs* : D *metuda es*, P *metuudaes* ; *maecti* : L *mehti*, DP *mechti* ; *end* : LDP *and* ; *-ȝidanc* : L *-ȝithanc*, D *gedeanc*, P *gedanc*.

(3) *uerc* : D *puerc*, P *puere* ; *uuldur-* : D *puldur*, P omits ; *fadur* : D *fudur* ; *sue* : DP *suae* ; *he* : D *hae* ; *uundra* : DP *pundra* ; *ȝihuaes* : L *ȝihuæs*, DP *gi-*.

(4) *dryctin* : M *y* made out of *i* and *c* out of *n*, D *drichtin*, P *drochtin*, *o* being deleted and *i* written over ; *astelidæ* : DP *astalde*.

(5) *aerist* : L *ærist*, D *uerst* with *a* over *u*, P *raeirst* ; *scop* : DP *scoop* ; *aelda* : L *ælda*, DP *eordu* ; *barnum* : M *barnŭ*, D *bearnum*, P *pearnum*.

(6) *heben* : L *hefen*, DP *efen* ; *til* : LDP *to* ; *hrofe* : L *hrofæ* ; *haleȝ* : L *haliȝ*, DP *halig* ; *scepen* : LDP *sceppend*.

---

(1) Gollancz (*The Cædmon Manuscript*, lxi) thinks that the opening word *Nu* might reflect the influence of some liturgy where the word referred to the Hour ; he also points out a tenth-century Benedictine Liturgy where the Office for each Hour began *We sculon God herian* (E. Thompson, *Select Monuments of Doctrine and Worship of the Catholic Church in England*, 1875, p. 113) ; cf also

CÆDMON'S HYMN

West Saxon Version

(MS Hatton, 43)

Nu pe sculan herian   heofonrices peard,
metudes myhte   7 his modȝeþanc,
3 purc puldorfæder,   spa he pundra ȝehpilc,
ece drihten,   ord astealde ;
he ærest ȝesceop   ylda bearnum
6 heofon to hrofe,   haliȝ scyppend,

Bouterwek, *Cædmon's des ags. biblische Dichtungen*, ccxxii. On the ellipsis of the pronoun *we*, cf *supra* p. 4, note 1.

(5) *aelda* : cf Bede's *filiis hominum* ; on DP *eordu*, cf *supra* p. 2.

(6) *scepen* : the second half-line is metrically imperfect (cf Sievers, ESt xliv. 295) and would have been so in the original unless *scepen* is a mistake for *sceppend* which appears in all other MSS including the closely related L. It is possible that *sceppend* has been replaced by another word OE *scepen (WGerm *skapinaȝ), which Schücking (ESt xliv. 155) sees in Beow. 106 *scyppend* (where *d* has been added by a later scribe, cf J. Zupitza, *Autotypes of Beowulf*, p. 6) and in Kt *sceppen* with *pp* due to the influence of the verb *sceppan* ; but the latter may be a Kt development of *sceppend*, as *beccen* is for *becgend*, *wrehten* for *wrehtend* (cf Kluge, IF vi. 341), and in the case of Beow. *scyppen* it is as easy to suppose the omission of final *d* (corrected by the later scribe) as to suppose the analogical addition of *p* in a form unrecorded outside CH *scepen*. A formal parallel to such a word *scepen* is found in OHG *scaffin*, *sceffin*, Fris *sheppena*, but the meaning of such words, 'juryman', is far from that required here (cf Sievers, *l.c.*). In view of the absence of any independent support for an OE *scepen* (the meaning of which would in any case be doubtful in the context) and the fact that all other MSS of CH agree on *sceppend*, it is perhaps better to regard *scepen* as being only a scribal variant (so Förster, *Lesebuch*, 3).

4

    tha middunȝeard   moncynnæs uard;
    eci dryctin   æfter tiadæ
9   firum foldu,   frea allmectiȝ.
Primo cantauit Caedmon istud carmen.

(7) *tha* : D *da*, P *dā* ; *middunȝeard* : M the first *d* altered from *n*, L *middinȝard*, DP *middumgeard* ; *-cynnæs* : DP *-cinnes* ; *uard* : DP *peard*.

(8) *eci* : D *éci* ; *dryctin* : D *drintinc*, P *drihtim* ; *æfter* : D *efter*, P *aefter* ; *tiadæ* : M *ti* made out of *d*, DP *tiade*.

(9) *foldu* : M *u* added above the line, D *onfoldu*, L *olfoldu* ; *-mectiȝ* : L *-mehtiȝ*, DP *-mechtig*.

(10) LDP omit.

---

(7) *tha* is correlative to *aerist* in line 5 (cf Bede *primo . . . dehinc . . .*). It is probable that *eci dryctin* begins a new sentence which simply expands the preceding one and which is entirely omitted by Bede's Latin paraphrase (*supra* p. 1) : " the Eternal Lord, the Almighty Ruler, afterwards adorned the earth for men "

middanȝearde   mancynnes þeard ;
ece drihten   æfter tida
9 firum on foldum,   frea ælmyhtiȝ.

In that case, *monncynnæs uard* is in apposition to *haleȝ scepen*, and *middunȝeard* is the object of *scop* and parallel to *heben*. It is not likely that *foldu* (line 9) is gen.sg. as Frampton (MPh xxii. 7, 9) suggests (cf *supra* p. 3 and p. 35, § 18*a*).

(8) *tiadæ* from **teogan* (Förster, Girvan § 432, note 2). On the ending *-adæ* cf *supra* p. 33, § 15.

(9) *foldu* : *-u* is a kind of shallow *v* added above the line. Förster (*Lesebuch* 4, note) interprets this superscribed *v* as an incomplete abbreviation mark ∼ and expands as *-un*, on account of forms like *scylun, middun-*, where final *-n* is kept (cf also Archiv cxxxv. 284). But the shallow superscribed *v* is used for *u* in LVD (Surtees Soc. Facsimile, fol. 34*b*) in the name *biuuulf*, and in CH(L) the reading is *foldu* (despite Miss Dobiache-Rojdestvensky's emendation to *foldun*) ; on the early loss of final *-n* cf *supra* p. 33, § 14.

BEDE'S DEATH SONG

Northumbrian Version

(MS St Gall 254, p. 253)

. . . et in *nost*ra quoq*ue* lingua ut erat doctus in nostris
carminib*us*, dicens de *te*rribili exitu animarum e corpore,

> Fore them neidfaerae   naenig uuiurthit
> thoncsnotturra   than him tharf sie,
> 3 to ymbhycggannae,   aer his hiniongae,
> huaet his gastae,   godaes aeththa yflaes,
> 5 aefter deothdaege   doemid uueorthae.

Cantabat *etiam* antiphonas ob *nost*ram consolationem. . . .

VARIANT READINGS: (1) A *the'*, B *thae*, EIL *the*; L *neyd-*;
E *facre*; L *vüiurthit*.

(2) I *tonc-*; E *-snottura*; *tharf*, A *f* written above *r*, E *thraf*,
L *thars*; I *sie̜*.

(3) B *-hycgganne̜*, I *-icggannae*; *hiniongae*, A *a* written above *e*.

(4) E *huaex*; EIL *gaste*; E *godeles*; AB *aꝙhtha*, EIL *aeththa*.

(5) EL *aester*; E *deoht*; E *doemit*, L *doemnl*; I *uueorthe*, L
vueorthe.

---

(1) All editors but Professor M. Förster have read the MS *the'*
(the mark is over *e*) as *there*, believing *-faerae* (which Symeon
wrongly translates *exitum*) to be from *faru* fem.ō-stem ' journey '.
Förster (*Lesebuch* 54) takes it to be from OE *fǽr* masc. 'sudden
danger' (cf Beow. 1068), that is, 'death'. He also points out (*op. cit.* 8)
that the sign ꝛ (usually for *er* or *re*) is otherwise unknown in the MS
and must be interpreted, like other cases which he notes in Archiv

42

BEDE'S DEATH SONG

Later Version

(MS Cotton Titus A II)

. . . et in nostra quoque lingua, hoc est anglica, ut erat doctus in nostris carminibus nonnulla dixit. Nam et tunc hoc anglico carmine componens multumque compunctus aiebat,

> For ðam neodfeore   næniᵹ peorðeð
> ðances snotora   ðonne him ðearf sy,
> 3 to ᵹehycᵹenne,   ær his heonenᵹanᵹe,
> hpæt his ᵹaste,   ᵹodes oððe yfeles,
> æfter deaðe heonen   demed peorðe.

Quod ita Latine sonat, Ante necessarium exitum prudentior quam opus fuerit nemo existit, ad cogitandum, videlicet antequam hinc proficiscatur anima, quid boni uel mali egerit, qualiter post exitum iudicanda fuerit. Cantabat etiam antiphonas secundum nostras consuetudines. . . .

---

cxxxv. 282, as a general mark of abbreviation. This would avoid the need for supposing a change in grammatical gender in the later versions. On the form *them* (for *thaem*) cf *supra* p. 31 § 9c note.

(3) On *-iongae* cf *supra* p. 28, § 5b; cf Judith *æfter hinsiðe*.

(4) " (to consider . . .) what good or evil may be decided for his soul after the day of death."

THE LEIDEN RIDDLE

Northumbrian Version

(MS Leiden, Voss 106, fol. 25b)

Mec se ueta uonʒ   uundrum freoriʒ
ob his innaðae   aerest cændæ.
3 *Ni* uaat ic mec biuorhtæ   uullan fliusum,
herum ðerh hehcraeft   hyʒiðonc*um min.*
Uundnae me ni biað ueflæ,   ni ic uarp hafæ,
6 ni ðerih ðreatun ʒiðraec   ðret me hlimmith,

---

(1) *ueta uonʒ*: there is space for two letters after *ueta* (Sweet, Kern) ; Schlutter first read *erð*, later *eorð*, but *r* occupies great lateral space so that there can hardly be room here for *erð* (cf Kern) ; Bethman read *m*, Pluygers *n(e)* or *n(ae)*, and Holthausen rightly read *na*. As this part of the text is clear there can be no doubt that these two much-faded letters have been erased, as Sweet suggests. Cf Exeter Book.

(2) *aerest* (so Dietrich, Sweet doubtfully, but clear with ultra-violet light) ; *aerist* (Schlutter, Kern doubtful and Sweet very doubtful). — *cændæ*: *cæn.æ* by ordinary vision, only *cæ...* by u.v. light. Bethman omits, Dietrich *c....*, Pluygers *ca(m)* or *ca(ð)*, Schlutter *cæ...*, Kern *cæ(nd.)*.

(3) *Uaat*, clear with u.v. but by ordinary vision it appears as *Uuat* (so Bethman, Dietrich, &c.) ; Schlutter saw traces of a *Ni* before *uuat.* — *biuorthæ* MS (*sic* for *biuorhtæ*, cf Exeter Book). LR' is fem.acc.sg., Exeter Book masc. The gender of the answers to the riddles often fluctuates (cf Wyatt, *OE Riddles* xxxv) ; *biuorthæ* would be correct for the answer *byrne* f.n-stem, ' coat of mail '.

(4) *herum* : MS *herū.* — *hehcraeft*: Schlutter alone differs in reading *haeh-*, but there is neither room for, nor any trace of, *a* squeezed in. — *hyʒiðoncum min* (completed from Exeter Book) ; only *hyʒiðonc* is now visible by u.v., the *h* being altered from *b*, and *c* over the line ; Pluygers read *b(i)giðo(cumt)*, Sweet *..gi(d.can.)* and Kern *h.ʒiðo..* ; Schlutter made out *huʒiðohta vFN* (v.l. *hFʒi-*), but the state of the MS does not justify it ; in any case uncials

44

WEST SAXON RIDDLE

Later Version

(Exeter Book, fol. 109a)

   Mec se pæta þonӡ   þundrum freoriӡ
   of his innaðe   ærist cende.
3 Ne þat ic mec beþorhtne   þulle flysum,
   hærum þurh heahcræft   hyӡeþoncum min.
   Þundene me ne beoð wefle,   ne ic þearp hafu,
6 ne þurh þreata ӡeþræcu   þræd me ne hlimmeð,

---

are only rarely used in the earlier folios of the MS and not at all in those parts of the OE riddle which are clear.

(5) *uundnae*, the ppt. is not usually inflected in OE when used predicatively ; *me . . . biað* is possessive, " I have no twisted woofs." — *hafæ* (so Schlutter) ; the MS is clear by u.v. (*hefæ* by Bethman, Pluygers, Sweet).

(6) *ðreatun* : on the form of this word cf *supra* p. 35, § 18c note. — *ðreatun ӡiðraec* : the greater part of *t* has been rubbed away, but if the MS is observed from the side the mark of *t* is still clear (visually and by u.v.) ; only Schlutter has read a letter here, first *ðreaunӡiðraec*, later *ðraevunӡiðraec*, but *v* is not used in the minuscule ; presumably this is for a compound *ðreawung-giðraec*, which Schlutter renders ' tortile opus ', but as Kern points out, *ðreauung* means ' correptio, castigatio, correctio ' and *ӡiðraec* does not mean ' opus ' but ' onrush, attack '. Taken literally, the sentence would mean " there is no thread in me which can resound through the onrush of troops " (that is, in battle) ; but it may have a more figurative sense " through the violence of its blows " in allusion to the passing of the thread backwards and forwards in the loom. — *ðret*, MS *ðrϕ* (Deitrich, Kern, &c.) ; Pluygers and Schlutter both mistook the ampersand for *æ*, reading *ðræ* and *ðræ'* (*sic* for *ðræd*) respectively. ϕ is however used elsewhere for the letters *et*, as in *uaϕeraelfinn'* (*supra* p. 7, n. 4), BDS *aeththa* &c. On the form *ðret* cf *supra* p. 27, § 2.

LEIDEN RIDDLE

Ne me hrutendu   hrisil scelfath,
ni mec ouana   aam sceal cnyssa.
9 Uyrmas mec ni auefun   uyrdi craeftum,
ða ði ʒeolu ʒodueb   ʒeatum fraetuath.
Uil mec hueþrae suaeðeh   uidæ ofaer eorðu
12 hatan mith heliðum   hyhtlic ʒiuæde ;
Ni anoeʒun ic me aeriʒfaerae   eʒsan brogum
ðeh ði numen siæ   niudlicae ob cocrum.

---

(7) *hrutendu* (so Bethman) ; the last letter is clearly *u* (Sweet, Pluygers), despite Dietrich's *-i* and Schlutter's *-e* (also read doubtfully by Kern). Sweet read a short tick adjoining the top of the following *h* as a nasal stroke, but if this is not a serif it may be part of an erased letter (so Schlutter). — *hrisil*, like MHG *risel* ' twig ' was probably a neut.*a*-stem ; elsewhere the OE word occurs only in glosses, so that besides the n.sg. *hrisl* (Corpus 1704), acc.sg. *hrisl, hrisil* (Epinal, Erfurt 851), dat.sg. *hrisle* (Corp. 713 = *ebredio* for *ab radio*), and dat.pl. in the phrase *hrislum hristlendum* (= *radiis stridentibus,* Wright-Wülcker's Vocab. ii. 83), the complete paradigm is not known. The neut.n.pl. would be *hris(i)l* and *hrutendu* (neut.n.pl. *ja*-stem) and *scelfath* (3pl.ind.pr.) would agree, though it should be pointed out that *scelfath* might possibly be a 3sg.form (cf Kolbe, § 199). The Exeter Book here (as in *amas,* line 8) changes the number of the noun, the adj. being made neut.sg. and a different vb. put in the 3sg. The Latin version is plural (*nec radiis carpor*). OE *hris(i)l* is invariably glossed by Lat. *radius* ' shuttle '. — *scelfath,* Pluygers *scel(p)at(h),* Bethman *scel.ad,* but others *scelfaeð* ; by ordinary vision the ending may equally well be *-aeð* or *-ath,* but by u.v. the latter is certain.

(8) *ouana* clear by u.v., though doubtful by ordinary vision (*ou..a*) ; Schlutter read *oua(n)a,* later *ahuana,* Sweet *ou(ua)n(a),* Pluygers *ou..ia.* — *aam,* a rare word which occurs as *aam* (Corpus 352, *haā* Epin. 177, *fam* Erfurt) ; Schlutter read *caam* (v.l. *cam a*). — *cnyssa* (Sweet, Pluygers, Kern, &c.) ; Schlutter *cnyissa(n),* but here *yi* is a misreading of the MS symbol for *y* (the second upper stroke of which turns down from the top almost to the lower line) and the final *-n* which he read when the page is held to the light is simply the *u* in *ceu* on the other side of the folio (cf Kern).

(9) *uyrdi* (so Bethman, Dietrich, Sweet) ; *uurdi* (Pluygers) ; Schlutter alone reads *uyndi, n* being a correction of *r,* but *r* is clear both by ordinary vision and u.v., with no trace of any correction. On *uyrdi* cf *supra* p. 34, § 17a.

WEST SAXON RIDDLE

ne æt me hrutende   hrisil scriþeð,
ne mec ohponan sceal   amas cnyssan.
9 Þyrmas mec ne apæfan   pyrda cræftum,
þa þe ʒeolo ʒodpebb   ʒeatpum frætpað.
Þile mec mon hpæþre se þeah   pide ofer eorþan
12 hatan for hæleþum   hyhtlic ʒepæde.
Saʒa soðcpidum,   searoþoncum ʒleap,
Þordum pisfæst,   hpæt þis ʒepædu sy.

(12) MS *ʒepædu*.

---

(10) MS *ʒeatŭ*.

(11) *hucthrae*, *h* being added above *t*, as is clear by u.v. (so Schlutter) ; MS *c* may be a faded *e*, and this *c* (or *e*) with *t* and the long downstroke of *h* has been misread as *d* (*hudrae* by Bethman, Dietrich, Sweet, Kern being doubtful about *d*). On the Nb form *huethrae* cf the Ruthwell Cross *hweþrae* (B. Dickins, *Leeds Studies in English* i. 18) and *v.* Girvan, § 359. On *c* for *e* cf Pluygers' form of *ʒiuæde* (line 12 *infra*).

(12) *ʒiuæde* (Sweet, Schlutter) ; Dietrich *giu(ae)..*, Pluygers *giu(æ)dc* ; the last letter is not now visible.

(13) *anoeʒun* : on the ending cf *supra* p. 35, § 18c ; Sedgefield would emend *anoeʒu nā ic.* — MS *broʒŭ*.

(14) *ðeh ði n...n siæ niudlicae :* this line is defective, but examination by ultra-violet light and u.v. photography reveals that the letter after the first *n* began with a minim (cf Bethman, Dietrich *ðim*, Pluygers *ði ni*) and that the word ends in *n* ; *siæ* is faint but clear by this light. The first word on the last line is *niudlicae* ; Pluygers had already read *maðlicae*, where the three minims are actually *ni*, *a* a confusion of *u* with the open *a* sometimes found (as in *uullan*, *eʒsan*), and *ð* a misreading of the uncrossed *ð* (found also here in *ʒodueb*). There is space for a few letters before *niudlicae* at the beginning of the last MS line but no trace of any letter now. The whole evidence would not be inconsistent with reading *ðeh ði numen siæ niudlicae ob cocrum* ' though it (the flight of arrows or each of the arrows) be eagerly taken from the quivers '. Dietrich first suggested *fracaðlicae* as a possibility and Rieger proposed reading the line *ðeh ði nimæn flanas fracaðlicae ob cocrum* as being a close enough rendering of the Latin *longis exempta faretris* ; much of this was read in the MS by Schlutter, who also read *lon(ʒum)* after *cocrum*, a suggestion which he later withdrew. But as already stated, the closest scrutiny of the MS reveals nothing to support such readings.

BIBLIOGRAPHY

1. BIBLIOGRAPHICAL LISTS

1883 R. Wülcker, in Grein-Wülcker's *Bibliothek* (*infra*).
1885 R. Wülcker, *Grundriss zur Geschichte der angelsächsischen Litteratur*, (CH 117–20, BDS 145).
1907 *Cambridge History of English Literature* I. 479–80.
1908 A. Brandl in *Grundriss der Germanischen Philologie*.
1910 G. Körting, *Grundriss der Geschichte der englischen Literatur* 45, (CH).
1913 R. Brotanek, *Texte und Untersuchungen zur altenglischen Literatur und Kirchengeschichte*, (BDS 151 ff).
1916 C. W. Kennedy, *The Cædmon Poems*, (CH 251 ff).
1931 A. H. Heusinkveld and E. J. Bashe, *A bibliographical Guide to Old English*, (CH 63–4, BDS 55 ; selective).

The following Bibliography includes only important articles and those not mentioned in the above bibliographical lists, and it refers *only* to the Northumbrian Poems.

2. FACSIMILES

1860 *Leiden Riddle :* F. Dietrich, *Kynewulfi Poetae Aetas.*
1879 *Cædmon's Hymn* (*Moore MS*) : Palaeographical Society, First Series, Vol. II, Part ii, Plate 140.
1913 *Bede's Death Song* (*St Gall*) : R. Brotanek, *Texte und Untersuchungen* (*supra*).
1928 *Cædmon's Hymn* (*Leningrad*) : Olga Dobiache-Rojdestvensky in Speculum III. 316.

3. EDITIONS

1705 T. Wanley, *Catalogus*, 287 (CH.M).
1722 *J. Smith, *Historia Ecclesiae Gentis Anglorum*, 597 (CH.M).
1826 *J. J. Conybeare, *Illustrations of Anglo-Saxon Poetry*, 6 (CH.M).
1832 B. Thorpe, *Cædmon's Metrical Paraphrase*, xxii (CH.M from Smith).
1844 *H. Hattemer, *Denkmäle des Mittelalters*, I, 3 (BDS.A).
1845 Bethmann, in ZfdA, v. 199 (LR).
1850 L. Ettmüller, *Engla and Seaxna Scopas and Boceras*, 25 (CH.M from Conybeare).

BIBLIOGRAPHY

1854 *K. W. Bouterwek, *Cædmon's des angelsächsischen biblische Dichtungen*, ccxxv (CH.M).

1857 C. W. M. Grein, *Bibliothek der angelsächsischen Poesie* (revised by Wülcker in 1883, see 1894-8 *infra*).

1860 *F. Dietrich, *Kynewulfi Poetae Aetas* (LR).

1861 *M. Rieger, *Alt- und angelsächsisches Lesebuch* (CH.M, BDS, LR).

1868 G. Stephens, *Runic Monuments*, ii. 435 (CH.M).

1869 G. Moberley, *Bedae Historia Ecclesiastica* (reprinted 1881), xvi (BDS.A).

1876 H. Sweet, *Anglo-Saxon Reader*, 195 (CH.M), seventh edition 1894, 175-6 (CH.M, BDS.A, LR) ; see 1922, Onions.

1876 *R. Wülcker, *Über den Hymnus Cædmons* in PBB iii. 348 ff, (CH.M).

1878 *J. Zupitza, in ZfdA xxii. 222 ff, (CH.M).

1879 *H. Bradshaw, Palaeographical Society (*supra*), (CH.M).

1881 J. E. B. Mayor and J. R. Lumby, *Bede's Historia Eccles.* 399, (BDS).

1881 J. Zupitza, *Altenglisches Übungsbuch*, (CH.M, BDS.A) (later editions, 5th by Schipper, 12th by Eichler 1921).

1885 *H. Sweet, *Oldest English Texts*, 148 ff, (CH.M, BDS.A, LR).

1888 F. Kluge, *Angelsächsisches Lesebuch*, 15, (CH.M), revised edition 1902-15, 103, (CH.M, BDS.A), 155, (LR after Sweet).

1890-8 *T. Miller, *The Old English Version of Bede's Ecclesiastical History*, ii. 597, (CH.M).

1894-8 Grein's *Bibliothek*, rev. by R. Wülcker, IIb. 7, (CH.M) and Assmann, IIIa. 205, LR (after Sweet).

1894 A. S. Cook, *A First Book in Old English*, 255, (BDS).

1896 *C. Plummer, *Baedae Opera Historica* I. clxi., (BDS.A, from Mayor and Lumby), II., 251, (CH.M).

1904 *P. Wuest, in ZfdA xlviii. 205 ff, (CH.DPM).

1909 *O. Schlutter, in Anglia xxxii. 384, also 1910 ib. xxxiii. 457, (LR).

1910 *F. Tupper, *Riddles of the Exeter Book*, 27, (LR after Sweet), 153, (LR after Schlutter).

1910 *J. H. Kern, in Anglia xxxiii. 453, also in 1914 Anglia xxxviii. 261, (LR).

1912 *A. J. Wyatt, *Old English Riddles*, 92, (LR after Schlutter).

1912 O. Schlutter, in Anglia xxxvi. 394, (BDS.A).

1913 *R. Brotanek, *Texte und Untersuchungen* (*supra*) 151 ff, (BDS all versions).

1913 *M. Förster, *Altenglisches Lesebuch*, 6, (CH.M, BDS.A).

1915 *M. Trautmann, *Die altenglischen Rätsel* 20, (LR).

1922 *C. T. Onions, revised edition of Sweet's *Anglo-Saxon Reader* 175, (CH.M. BDS.A ; LR, partly after Schlutter).

49

THREE NORTHUMBRIAN POEMS

1922 *W. J. Sedgefield, *An Anglo-Saxon Verse Book*, 80–1, (CH.M, BDS.A), 118, (LR).
1924 *M. G. Frampton, in MPh xxii. 1 ff, (CH.M).
1927 *Sir I. Gollancz, *The Cædmon Manuscript*, xi, (CH.M).
1928 *Olga Dobiache-Rojdestvensky, in Speculum iii. 316 ff, (CH.L).
1930 G. T. Flom, *Introductory Old English Grammar and Reader*, (CH.M, BDS.A, from Sweet).
1931 H. Naumann, *Frühgermanisches Dichterbuch* 127, (CH.M).

4. STUDIES AND NOTES

In addition to the works marked * in the preceding sections the following may be included here:

1832 Sir F. Palgrave, in *Archæologia* xxiv. 341 ff, (CH).
1854 J. Grimm, *Deutsche Mythologie* (translated by J. S. Stallybrass 1880), (CH).
1891 A. S. Cook, ' The name Cædmon ', in MLA vi. 9 ff, (CH).
1899 H. M. Chadwick, *Studies in Old English* 1899, (Language).
1902 A. S. Cook, *Notes on the Ruthwell Cross* in MLA xvii. 367 ff, (Language).
1905 A. Schroer, Archiv cxv. 67–9, (CH).
1913 G. Sarrazin, *Von Kädmon bis Kynewulf*, 17 ff, (CH).
1914 Blanche C. Williams, *Gnomic Poetry in Anglo-Saxon*, 67–9, (BDS).
1915 K. Wildhagen in Archiv cxxxiv. 175 (rev. of Brotanek), (BDS).
1916 M. Förster, in Archiv cxxxv. 282, (CH.M, BDS).
1926 Nellie S. Aurner, MLN xli. 535, (CH).
1927 F. Klaeber, MLN xlii. 390, (CH).
1927 A. S. Cook, Speculum II. 67 ff, (CH).
1929 Louise Pound, in *Studies in English Philology presented to F. Klaeber*, 232, (CH).
1929 E. Sievers, in *Britannica*, 57 ff, (CH).

5. TRANSLATIONS

1868 G. Stephens, *Runic Monuments*, II. 433, (CH).
1892 S. A. Brooke, *History of Early English Literature* 340, (BDS).
1902 A. S. Cook and C. B. Tinker, *Select Translations from Old English Poetry* (2nd edition 1926) 77–8, (CH, BDS).
1916 C. W. Kennedy, *The Cædmon Poems*, 3, (CH).
1918 C. Faust and S. Thompson, *Old English Poems*, 83–4, (CH).
1926 R. K. Gordon, *Anglo-Saxon Poetry* x, (CH), 332, (riddle 35).
1927 A. S. Cook, in Speculum II. 71, (CH).

Cf also the list of Abbreviations for works on language.

GLOSSARY

In the Glossary, words will be found under the forms in which they occur in the text, except that nouns and adjectives (excluding irregular comparatives, &c.) will be found under the nom.sg.(masc.) and verbs under the infinitive ; pronouns under the nom.sg.masc. (except in the case of the 1st and 2nd persons of the personal pronouns which will be found under the nom.sg. or nom.pl. as the case may be). Irregular grammatical or phonological forms will be noted in their proper alphabetical place with cross references to the words under which they are dealt with.

The order of letters is alphabetical : *ae* (*æ*) is treated as a separate letter after *a* ; *ð, th* after *t* ; *oe* after *o*. No distinction is made between *ð, th* ; between *u, uu* ; between *g* and *ʒ* ; or between *ae* and *æ*. The prefix *ge-* is always ignored in the arrangement of the glossary.

Abbreviations are the commonly accepted ones : n. = noun, neut. = neuter, p. = past, pt. = participle, t. = tense, v. = (strong) verb, w. = weak, &c., besides C = Cædmon's Hymn, B = Bede's Death Song and L = the Leiden Riddle. Reference is by poem (C, B or L) and line. When the line reference is followed by *n* the word is discussed in the footnotes *supra*, and when followed by * the word in the text is reconstructed or an emended form.

Reference is made to the New English Dictionary by printing the NED word (under which the OE word is discussed) as the first meaning in capitals ; if this word is not the true phonological descendant of the OE form in the glossary it is italicized. Unless it provides the exact meaning required by the context it is followed by a semicolon and the meaning required in ordinary lower case type. If it is radically different in meaning or if it is obsolete and archaic it is enclosed in square brackets.

A

allmectiʒ, *adj.* ALMIGHTY C9.

ām, *m.a-stem*, reed (of a loom) L8 (*aam*).

anoēg(n)an, *w.v.(1b)*, fear, dread L13n.

āstellan, *w.v.(1b)*, ordain C4.

āuefan, *v.(5)*, WEAVE L9.

Æ

aefter, *prep.(with dat.)*, AFTER B5 ; *adv.* afterwards C8.

aelde, *m.i-stem (pl.)*, men C5.

āēr, *prep.(with dat.)*, ERE, before B3.

āērist, -est, *adv.* [ERST] ; first C5, L2.

aeriʒ-faru, *f.ō-stem*, ARROW-flight, flying of arrows L13.

aeththa, *conj.* [OTHER] ; or B4.

B

barn, *n.a-stem*, [BAIRN] ; child, descendant C5.

bēon, *anom.v.* BE ; **bīað,** *pres. pl.ind.* L5 ; **sīe,** *sg.subj.* B2, L14.

biuorhtæ, *p.pt.* (*ƒ.acc.sg.*), [BE-WORKED] ; worked with, made of L3*.

brōga, *m.n-stem,* terror, fear L13.

C

cænnan, *w.v.*(*1b*), [KEN] ; bring forth L2*.

cnyssa, *w.v.*(*1a*), strike, knock L8.

cocer, *m.a-stem,* [COCKER] ; quiver L14.

craeft, *m.a-stem,* CRAFT ; skill, strength L9.

D

dēoth-daeg, *m.a-stem,* DEATH-DAY B5.

dōēman, *w.v.*(*1b*), DEEM : determine, decide B5.

dryctin, *m.a-stem,* [DRIGHTIN] ; lord C4, 8.

E

eci, *adj.* [ECHE] ; eternal C4, 8.

egsa, *m.n-stem,* peril (*gen.sg.*) L13.

end, *conj.* AND C2.

eorðe, *ƒ.n-stem,* the EARTH, (*acc.sg.*) L11.

F

fīras, *m.ja-stem* (*pl.*), men C9.

flīus, *n.i-stem,* FLEECE L3.

folde, *ƒ.n-stem,* [FOLD] ; the earth, (*acc.sg.*) C9n.

fore, *prep.*(*with dat.*), before B1.

fraetwan, *w.v.*(*1b*), [FRET] ; adorn L10.

frēa, *m.n-stem,* ruler, lord C9.

frēoriȝ, *adj.* cold L1.

G

gāst, *m.a-stem,* GHOST ; soul, spirit, (*dat.sg.*) B4.

ȝeatwe, *ƒ.wō-stem* (*pl.*), ornaments ; **ȝeatum,** *dat.pl.* used *adv.* with splendour, splendidly L10.

ȝeolu, *adj.* YELLOW, (*neut.acc. sg.*) L10*.

gōd, *n.a-stem,* GOOD B4.

ȝodueb, *n.ja-stem,* [GOD + WEB] ; fine precious cloth, silk, (*acc.sg.*) L10.

H

habban, *w.v.*(*3*), HAVE L5.

hāleȝ, *adj.* HOLY C6.

hātan, *v.*(*7*), [HIGHT] ; call L12.

hē, *pron.* HE C3 &c. ; **his,** *gen.sg.* his C2 ; **him,** *dat.sg.* for him B2.

heben, *m.a-stem,* HEAVEN C6.

hefaenrīce, *n.ja-stem,* [RICHE] ; the kingdom of HEAVEN C1.

hēhcraeft, *m.a-stem,* HIGH skill L4.

heliŏ, *m.þ-stem,* man, hero L12.

hēr, *n.a-stem,* HAIR L4.

herȝan, *w.v.*(*1a*), praise C1.

hiniong, *m.a-stem,* [HEN-sith, YONG] ; departure, death B3.

hlimman, *v.*(*3*), resound L6.

hrīsil, *n.a-stem,* shuttle L7n.

hrōf, *m.a-stem,* ROOF C6.

hrūtan, *v.*(*2*), [ROUT] ; roar, resound, (*pres.pt.neut.pl.*) L7n.

ȝihwā, *pron.* each C3.

huaet, *pron.neut.* WHAT B4.

huethre, *conj.* WHETHER ; *h. suaeðeh,* however, nevertheless L11*.

hyȝiŏonc, *m.a-stem,* [HIGH + THANK] ; thought L4*.

hyhtlic, *adj.* [HIGHT-] ; joyful, pleasant, (*neut.acc.*) L12.

I

ic, *pron.* I L3, &c. ; **mec,** *acc.*

me Lĭ, &c., myself L3 ; **me,**
L6, 7, &c.; **min,** *gen.* of me,
mine L4*; **me,** *dat.* for (in)
me, myself L5, 6, 13.

innað, *m.a-stem,* [INNETH] ;
inside, womb L2.

M

maect, *f.i-stem,* MIGHT, power
(*acc.pl.*) C2.

metud, *m.a-stem,* God, Creator
C2.

middunȝeard, *m.a-stem,* [MID-
DENERD]; the earth C7.

mith, *prep.(with dat.),* [MID] ;
with, amongst L12.

modȝidanc, *m.a-stem,* [MOOD
+ THANK] ; thought, under-
standing C2.

moncynn, *n.ja-stem,* [MANKIN] ;
mankind C7.

N

nāeniȝ, *pron.* no one B1.

ne, *v.* **ni.**

nēid-fǽr, *m.a-stem,* [NEED +
FEAR] ; the inevitable, sudden
peril, death B1.

ni, *adv.* not L3*, 13, &c. ; *conj.*
nor L5, &c., **ne** L7.

nīudlicae, *adv.* eagerly L14.

nū, *adv.* NOW C1.

O

ob, *prep.(with dat.)* OF ; out of,
from L2, 14.

ofaer, *prep.(with acc.),* OVER
L11.

ōr, *n.a-stem,* [ORE] ; beginning
origin C4.

ōuana, *adv.* from anywhere L8.

S

sceal, *v.* **sculan.**

scelfan, *v.(3),* shake, reverber-
ate L7.

scepen, *m.a-stem,* [SHEPPEND]
Creator C6n.

sceppan, *v.(6),* SHAPE ; create
C5.

sculan, *anom.v.* be obliged,
shall ; **sceal,** *3sg.pres.ind.*
L8 ; **scylun,** *1pl.* C1.

sĕ, *dem.pron.* and *def.art.m.,*
that, the L1 ; **thĕm,** *m.dat.*
B1 ; **ðā,** *n.pl.* those L10.

sīe, *v.* **bēon.**

suāēðĕh, *conj.* yet ; *v.* **huethre.**

suĕ, *conj.* as, even as C3.

ᛁᛖᚱᛞ

T

*****tēogan,** *w.v.(2),* make, create,
tiadæ, *p.t.* C8n.

til, *prep.* [TILL]; to; (*with dat.*)
as, for C6.

tō, *prep.(with acc.),* TO B3.

TH Ð

thā, *adv.* [THO] ; then C7.

than, *conj.* THAN B2.

tharf, *f.ō-stem,* [THARF] ; need
B2.

ðĕh, *conj.* THOUGH, although ;
ð. ði L14.

ðer(i)h, *prep.(with acc.),*
THROUGH, by L4, 6.

ði, *part. v.* **ðĕh.**

ði, *rel.pron.(n.pl.),* who, which
L10.

thoncsnottur, *adj.* wise in
thought B2.

ȝiðraec, *n.a-stem,* pressure,
violence L6.

ðrēat, *m.a-stem,* THREAT; pressure; ? weight L6n.

ðrēt, *m.a-stem.* THREAD L6.

U, UU

uard, *m.a-stem,* [WARD] ; guar-
dian, protector C1, 7.

uarp, *n.a-stem,* WARP L5.

uãt, *pret.pres.(1),* [WOT] ; know L3 (*uaat*).

ȝiuæde, *n.ja-stem,* [WEED] ; garment L12*.

uefl, *f.ō-stem,* woof L5.

uueorthan, *v.(3),* [WORTH] ; be, become ; (*3sg.pres.ind.*) B1, (*3sg.pres.subj.*) B5.

uerc, *n.a-stem,* WORK C3.

uẽt, *adj.* WET, damp L1.

uïdæ, *adv.* widely, far L11.

uillan, *anom.v.* WILL, (*3sg.*) L11n.

uonȝ, *m.a-stem,* [WONG] ; meadow, field L1.

uuldur-fæder, *m.r-stem,* FATHER of glory, (*gen.sg.*) C3.

uulle, *f.n-stem,* WOOL L3.

uunden, *p.pt.* WOUND, twisted, turned, (*n.pl.*) L5n.

uundor, *n.a-stem,* WONDER, marvel C3.

uundrum, *adv.* wondrously, strangely L1.

uyrd, *f.i-stem,* [WEIRD] ; fate, (*gen.sg.*) L9 (cf Introd.).

uyrm, *m.i-stem,* WORM, silkworm L9.

Y

yfel, *n.a-stem,* EVIL B4.

ymbhycȝgan, *w.v.(3),* consider, think B3.

INDEX